The Theatre Student

PRODUCING PLAYS FOR CHILDREN

Theatre for children by youth offers a challenge to both actors and stage technicians and stimulates performers and audience alike to an active play of imagination. The two "gremlins" shown here are high-school players, appearing on the surface of the moon—as envisioned by teen-age designers who created this setting for The Man in the Moon.

The Theatre Student

PRODUCING PLAYS FOR CHILDREN

Richard C. Johnson

with drawings by David Shurte

PUBLISHED BY

RICHARDS ROSEN PRESS, INC.
NEW YORK, N.Y. 10010

Standard Book Number: 8239–0225–0
Library of Congress Catalog Card Number: 73–134902
Dewey Decimal Classification: 792

Published in 1971 by Richards Rosen Press, Inc.
29 East 21st Street, New York City, N.Y. 10010

First Edition

Manufactured in the United States of America

TO GLADIE AND BILL

CONTENTS

ACKNOWLEDGMENTS

Most of the plays pictured were directed by the author. Robert H. Keil and Ada Mary Hunt directed *Alice in Retrospect,* and Mr. Keil was technical director for *The Sleeping Beauty, The Tinder Box, The Puppet Prince,* and *Pygmalion.* Robert S. Ploch directed *The Magic Isle,* and was technical director for *Greensleeves' Magic, The Man in the Moon,* and *Once Upon a Mattress.* The director of *Antigone* was Hayward Ellis.

PREFACE

Good theatre for children is an exciting experience—exciting because it turns us from our self-concerns and lifts us to a level of involvement beyond ourselves. By reaching out to share experiences, we realize more fully our own capacities to imagine and to respond. And so we grow.

This growth is realized by both the theatre student and the child audience. Each grows a little bigger through the experience—reaching to greater heights of imagination from roots more deeply planted in truth.

Richard C. Johnson
Barrington, Illinois

"To give a fair chance to potential creativity," wrote Arnold Toynbee, "is a matter of life and death for any society." Whether such a statement is applied to parents in the home, enjoying and encouraging the imagination of their children, to a business that rewards its employees with promotions in return for creative ideas, or to a society that supports the arts, the meaning is the same. So it is a matter for rejoicing when a high-school drama department engages in the creative activity of providing good theatre for the children in its community.

Because so many cities and towns at present are without theatres for child audiences, it is especially important that a good high-school drama department in the district produce at least one play for children each year. If a director is tentatively interested in such a project, let him read the author's Prologue to this book to be convinced! Then read on and find out what such a venture involves, for the book is written by a director of many years' experience and is entirely practical in every aspect of the project. It will save a person who is not experienced in theatre for children from countless mistakes he is sure to make without such advice.

Children, although exacting, are the most genuine audience in the world. They live in the story if it is well set forth, even the most sophisticated rejoicing when things go well for the hero; jeering at the pompous or villainous characters; and suddenly becoming so utterly silent in moments of suspense that one would think the darkened auditorium was empty! On the other hand, if an audience is bored by long or indistinct speeches of lack of action, it does not politely sit still like an adult audience but makes the players aware by buzzings and stirrings that something is wrong. Charlotte Chorpenning, at the Goodman Theatre in Chicago, used her audience as a laboratory to test her plays before they were published. That is why most of them have been so successful.

Many of the finest university and high-school actors delight in playing for children's theatre, especially when the plays are great stories such as *Tom Sawyer, Rip Van Winkle, Peter Pan,* and *Treasure Island,* with such wonderful characters as Long John Silver, Captain Hook, Nana, Muff Potter, Injun Joe, and others who challenge the most skilled players.

This book, I predict, will serve two very useful purposes; first, in arousing the interest of many high-school drama departments and youth organizations to make a beginning in the production of plays for child audiences; and second, in offering young people "a fair chance" to engage in a worthy and fascinating creative activity.

Winifred Ward

ABOUT THE AUTHOR

RICHARD C. JOHNSON is chairman of the Performing Arts Department, Barrington High School, Barrington, Illinois, and chairman of the Drama Department in the Georgia Governor's Honors Program.

Actively involved in educational theatre organizations, he is the First Assistant Director of the Secondary School Theatre Conference, a division of the American Educational Theatre Association. He has been a member of the American Educational Theatre Association Board of Directors, and has served both the Children's Theatre Conference and the Secondary School Theatre Conference as national program chairman.

In 1960 he was chairman of the educational theatre delegation to the White House Conference on Children and Youth, where he served as a workgroup leader. Following that meeting, he continued to represent educational theatre on the Council of National Organizations for Children and Youth, and he has served two terms on the executive committee of that organization.

Previous publications include articles appearing in *Dramatics,* the *Educational Theatre Journal, Clearing House,* and the *Illinois Journal of Education.* A series of articles appearing in *Dramatics* was reissued by the National Thespian Society under the title *Theatre for Children.* In collaboration with Robert C. Seaver, he prepared a widely used filmstrip, *Makeup for the Stage,* and an accompanying text entitled *A Guide to Makeup for the Stage.*

The days that make us happy
make us wise.

—John Masefield

The "generation gap" narrowed as a young admirer met a high-school actress after her perform-ance in The Elves and the Shoemaker. *They had shared a common joy in the children's theatre experience.*

PEOPLE IN THE THEATRE

This prologue to a book about theatre is about young people. It is a look into what makes them tick and why the theatre experience can be significant in their lives. Further, it is a look at their moment in history and their unique place in it. Before we concern ourselves directly with theatre for children by youth, I am inviting you to share with me in a search for insight into the behaviors and the learnings of both groups. But if you are anxious to get on with the specifics of children's theatre—to get the show on the road—perhaps you will want to skip this for now and come back to it at your leisure.

THEATRE AND YOUTH

At no time in history has there been a greater need for defining the role of youth in our society—both for himself and for the elders with whom he must interact. He resists being swallowed by and digested into the adult "establishment"—and if society suffers heartburn and seeks remedies, he may obediently quiet his resistance but he is no less confused. Or, even more disturbed by his role, he may rebel.

The human spirit does not achieve its maximum creative, constructive potential under controls imposed from outside itself. Discipline in the most functional sense is self-imposed, motivated by a response to need. It has little to do with fear-motivated obedience.

Please understand, this is not a defense of rebellious youth. Rebellion occurs in one whose resistance has been misunderstood and, therefore, aggravated to a point of climax. Fear, which might have motivated obedience, is overthrown in a dramatic moment of bravado. At such a moment the human spirit is sick and crying; it is not speaking out firmly from a position of strength. The psychologist might say one is "acting out" his aggressions.

"Acting out" seems to be a fundamental human experience. Whether we respond to fear or to more aggressive motivations, we behave—or *act*—with or without self-imposed disciplines, depending upon the nature of our learnings during the years when our habits of response are being developed.

That has always been true, of course, but it is a matter of greater social concern during this moment in history because society is changing so rapidly. Earlier in this century, a person might grow up learning his role by following in the footsteps of a parent. He was secure in the knowledge that the same value systems, the same patterns of work and leisure, the same husband-wife-

21

child relationships, the same religious activity, and often even the same specific vocation would accurately define his adult role.

Now those old ways, which seemed to be naturally self-perpetuating, have largely disappeared from the social scene. Rather than having the assurance that what he observes and acts out in imitation of his elders will be his adult role, present-day youth has only the assurance that the society he observes is *not* the society in which he will live—that the role models he observes are *not* the roles he will play in his adult life.

Because that is true, young people are more inclined to find role models among their peers—models of adaptability to change. They find exemplars among their elders only insofar as they do not appear to be rooted in the past but, rather, move with self-assurance toward an uncertain future.

For self-assurance to be more than mere bluff—whether in a peer model or an adult—it must stem from a firm foundation in *truth*. Values, institutions, and technologies may change, but *truth* is a constant. In fact, evolving social changes viewed in historical perspective can provide ever deepening insights into *fundamental truth*.

At this point we might ask, where do we seek this fundamental element? If we as young persons or adults would serve well as exemplars—or if, indeed, we would seek order in our own lives during this time of accelerated change—where do we turn to find truth?

The artist throughout our evolving civilization has been identified as the man of insight, having means and materials for communicating his unique revelation to those who could interpret his symbols. He has spoken to men in his own time and, on universal themes, has reached beyond his own time to enrich unborn generations. He has spoken his insights in the rhythm and melody of music and dance, in color and form on canvas or in clay, and in the language, action, and spectacle of the theatre.

Of all the arts, the theatre speaks its truths most directly in terms relevant to the behaviors that define our life roles. Because its basic materials—voice, body, and sensory-emotional resources—are held in common by all mankind, it can involve all people of any age in the search for truth and can provide the self-discipline necessary for moving easily from one role to another. Role-playing on the stage, as in life, requires that characters be effectively motivated, that they listen and respond to others, and that they face the social consequences of their action. Within this pattern of experience lies *truth*.

To discover fundamental truths in a variety of social settings would seem not only a significant but an essential experience for one who would live well in a society that promises a lifetime of technological and social change. When one discovers that *truth* is rooted in himself, not in any social structure or value system, he is not likely to rebel or to retreat in the face of change.

May I suggest that there are two good ways to make that discovery. One is to live a lifetime richly varied in challenges and responses.

> All the world's a stage . . .
> And one man in his time plays many parts.

We might expect that one who has lived out his time would, by trial and error, have achieved some insight. The alternative would be to shortcut the full life with its "many parts"—to reverse the image in Shakespeare's view of man and find that the stage is a window to all the world, revealing truths that are not of a time or place, but of the universal human experience.

Realizing that participation in role-playing experiences is important education for life in the world beyond the theatre in no way negates the fun of involvement—nor does it dilute the importance of theatre as an art. The artist, in fact, is more ready to live—and has more fun—than the person who has never learned to exercise his imagination in embracing new experiences. Moreover, such positive gains are born of his willingness to say, "The play's the thing," to submerge *self* in seeking *art*. He grows stronger and more versatile in living as he accepts the disciplines of a performing artist.

To assist in the personal growth and aesthetic awareness of young people, adults and adult institutions must recognize needs implied in the behaviors of youth and assume responsibility for meeting them. Although one's aimless or destructive behavior may suggest a need for activities that will "keep him off the street," this negative interpretation takes a shallow view of his true potential.

Every normal human creature has a vast untapped potential for *competence*. He is an intellectual being, capable of understanding and logical thought; he is a physical being, capable of purposeful action; he is a sensory being, capable of lively imagination; he is an emotional being, capable of powerful feelings; and he has the potential capability of employing all of those resources as he views experiences objectively and subjectively to form critical and aesthetic judgments.

The truly educated person is one who has learned to make controlled use of all those capacities so that his life and his art reflect competence born of such control. He is not the "brain" who lacks imagination to make creative use of his knowledge or the skilled athlete who "blows up" in response to an unfavorable ruling by an official. Nor is he the poet or actor who gives way to a display of maudlin sentiment or a gross exhibition of self. He is one who maintains a purposeful balance in the use of his powers and, in so doing, enjoys the excitement that attends the pursuit of competence.

Those who would work with young people and the organizations they build must provide self-fulfilling activities, which Roy Sorenson has called the "challenge of competence." He called for "a spirit of experimentation" approached "sensitively and imaginatively; . . . enrichments to the teen-age culture rather than assaults upon it." [1]

The theatre experience provides that kind of enrichment. In it the young performer finds a constant challenge demanding that he adapt to each new role and situation intellectually, physically, imaginatively, and emotionally. He learns that there is no limit to his competence, that there are only new

---

[1] Roy Sorenson, *Youth's Need for Challenge and Place in American Society: Its Implications for Adults and Adult Institutions*, National Committee for Children and Youth, Washington, 1962.

levels and new challenges. He learns to see art and life as open-ended—filled with the excitement of creative experimentation.

Young people working in the theatre at any level can meet great challenges and grow to great heights in responding to them. But youth in theatre for children have a very special challenge—a very special opportunity. Not only are they taking a great stride in developing their own creative potential, but they are introducing the values of a theatre experience to a new generation.

Probably at no time in our lives are we more capable of intense commitment than teen-time. Young people will seek and follow a role model with a zeal that makes adult enthusiasms seem uninspired by comparison. Given the opportunity *and a cause,* they can lead with the same kind of excited involvement. Once they realize the worth of what they are doing in children's theatre, they can become a truly significant community resource.

THEATRE AND CHILDREN

Much of the process by which we educate the young is additive. That is, we find ways of *adding* to the existing fund of knowledge and experience. Of equal importance, I believe, is finding ways of *preserving, nourishing,* and *vitalizing* the content of that fund and of avoiding the negative experiences that can shrink interest and deny the potential for growth.

One of childhood's richest resources is *imagination.* There is no telling what heights a child might reach through imaginative experimentation if adults and adult institutions would cease to punish and discourage the free play of imagination. For one to achieve his maximum potential, he must retain the power to dream in all directions. He must be able imaginatively to recreate past knowledge and experiences, to involve his senses empathically in the experiences of others, and to dream beyond what he knows and has observed.

Creative play-making is a part of the young child's normal experience. He makes little or no distinction between experiences of his own past or current life and those that are the pure product of an active imagination. Imaginary friends are commonplace, and they become important participants in each day's experience. Real and imagined people and events are accepted with the same unquestioning belief, and it is only the intrusion of adult reactions that ultimately pushes imagined experience to the periphery of sensory awareness and introduces the idea that what is real is more true than what is imagined.

With the introduction of that idea, imagination faces its greatest threat. Unless avenues remain open whereby imagination is encouraged to travel beyond the realities of each day's routines, it falls far behind the intellectual and physical development attained by the child as he grows toward maturity. And without the balance and control that a flexible imagination can provide, emotional discipline is left purely to chance or the rule of fear. The result is a potentially explosive force by which one may hurt those he would wish to help or destroy his own potential for a creative life.

The problem is particularly acute among the overcrowded and underprivileged children of the city. Theirs is a compelling need for exciting flights of imagination away from the oppressive, frightening, dehumanizing realities.

Without their dreams, they grow out of touch with joy and have nothing toward which to hope and strive.

The theatre experience is one important means of sharing moments of joy and giving direction to dreams. Empathizing with others in their sorrows and pleasures, sharing their hopes and struggles, and knowing with them the essential truths revealed by those shared experiences have a uniquely humanizing effect.

Going to the theatre can encourage more dramatic play among children, not for an audience but for the self-discovery that grows out of role identification and imaginative experimentation. Hopefully, the time will come when all children will have organized training for active imagination through creative drama classes under trained adult leadership, and all children will know the theatre as a continuing source of joy and excitement in their lives.

It is toward that end that your venture into children's theatre is a significant step. The need is evident. The arts have marked the ascending path of civilization in every age and in every culture. The art of theatre—"as 't were, a mirror up to nature"—is the art that most clearly illuminates the human experience.

In a theatre of youth for children, everyone gains and nobody loses. The child audience gains new directions for imagination to travel—hopefully toward an adult life in which each may truly say, "I have a dream." The performers and production crew gain understandings, insights, and a higher sensitivity as well as a new sense of their own worth.

By responsibly meeting the many challenges that occur in the process of building a play production, they deny the widely advertised image of the teen-ager and, in fact, become a significant influence on a new generation, a source of inspiration for their elders, exemplars to their peers, and an asset to a growing American theatre tradition.

Chapter I

GETTING STARTED

Before picking up this book, you must have had some desire to bring children and youth together in a theatre experience so that both might gain something of value. If you were dedicated exclusively to serving the values inherent in cognitive learnings, you would not be reading this now. Perhaps for reasons discussed in the prologue or perhaps because you have experienced the excitement of children's theatre and know the satisfaction of working with young people, you are attracted to a book that suggests that these two imaginative and energetic groups can be brought together in a common theatre experience.

First, let us consider what have *not* been your reasons for interest in a children's theatre venture. You have not chosen it because you think high-school-age performers are incapable of anything "better." Any adult who works with young people must honestly respect them or his evidence of success will be limited to whatever he can contrive on paper. It will never be seen in their behavior on stage or off. For a theatre to achieve anything better than box-office objectives, the players must be respected by their director, and together they must work to earn the respect of their audience.

Another unworthy reason that sometimes leads groups into the production of plays for children is the mistaken notion that they are an uncritical audience—that anything goes and, therefore, that putting on a "kid show" is easy. Well, anything does not go! Keeping pace with the lively imaginations of children is no small assignment. If children are bored or offended by a conde-

scending attitude, they will find their own ways of delivering the message. They are a marvelous audience if approached in a proper spirit. But, like the players themselves, they must be respected if they are to perform well.

The foundation for that respect is the recognition by the entire production team that when they perform for children, they assume an important responsibility. In the children's theatre, they provide a significant aesthetic experience to a greater assembly of undiscovered and undeveloped *potential* than could be reached in any other audience. In the children's theatre audience are many imaginations that are still relatively free. The inhibiting experiences that threaten to stifle this rich resource are still ahead. As the walls of inhibition close in, potential leaders may become followers, potential inventors may become technicians, potential authors and actors may become salesmen, and potential audiences for a living theatre may become comfortably addicted to some perennial TV series or the reruns of old movies. The degree to which they will achieve their full potential for a creative life will depend on the manner in which their imaginations are nourished and encouraged *now*.

Realizing that your teen-age theatre company can share that kind of lofty objectives is one way of indicating your regard for youth and their generation. Once communication is established on such a plane of mutual respect, your young people are not likely to let you down. Children's theatre not only will involve their thoughts and imaginations in a rewarding creative activity, but, because it satisfies a need, can inspire a spirit of dedication. They probably would not have joined your group at all if they had not recognized some value in the theatre experience. As respected partners in the enterprise, they will be pleased to discuss its significance and to share your interest in using it to help develop the rich potential represented in your audience.

When the young people in your theatre consider the importance of meeting their audience and providing a needed experience, they will recognize, of course, that the theatre experience is only one of many that will help members of their audience to develop their creative potential. Whatever aesthetic experiences children have will be far too few, however, and your group will recognize the children's theatre as their opportunity to make one meaningful contribution.

All this, of course, assumes that the group already is organized and that you do not have a selling job to do before getting started. That assumption probably applies only to a limited number of readers. For many, the word *potential* as applied to the audience will apply to the youth group as well. The talent is there, but it may not have been discovered. The energy is there, but it may be dissipated without purpose as members pull in different directions. The spirit is there, but it may still be seeking a cause to serve.

If you would direct their spirit and energy and develop their talent to serve the cause of children's theatre, the best first step is to involve young people vicariously by visiting a good production of a play for children. Enjoying a good performance and observing the reactions of an excited audience of children can say more about the worth of the experience than could be told in a dozen lectures. The theatre experience itself is the best resource for a discussion of values that will help to focus your group's attention on goals.

One word of caution, however: Be sure that the first exposure is *good theatre*. Just any play for children is not good enough. Regrettably, many performing groups are meeting audiences of children with play productions that are offensively condescending in content or style or are theatrically ineffective in performance.

Bad theatre exists for a number of reasons. Most obvious, I suppose, is the failure of producing organizations to establish good theatre as a goal. If the primary motivation is making money, either for personal gain or to finance some project unrelated to the theatre experience, more imagination and energy may be devoted to a promotion campaign than to the preparation of a worthy performance.

Another roadblock in the path of good theatre is failure to appreciate the significance of the theatre experience for both the audience and the performing group. By an artless perversion of purpose, the performer may seek to exhibit himself rather than to share an aesthetic experience. Your group should be introduced to children's theatre by witnessing an exciting, purposeful performance, not an ego-centered display.

Or perhaps a group performing for children fails to appreciate the audience, assuming that children are uncritical in their response to entertainment. Your players will learn nothing constructive by visiting a theatre that does not take pride in presenting a quality theatre experience to a deserving audience.

Participants in good theatre give emphasis to the creative use of imagination and realize a sense of personal growth that gains in depth as it is shared in performance. There is no terminal point to such growth if the theatre functions dynamically as an avenue to new insights, suggesting new directions for the imagination to travel. The spirit of good theatre is contagious and can inspire your people to a good start.

Although some excellent professional children's theatres exist, professional status offers no assurance of excellence in performance. Some players are professional only in the sense that they depend upon the theatre as a source of income. Finding a good professional group near enough to be visited may be impossible for you, but many university, high-school, and community theatres offer quality performances equal to the best of the professionals. They should be investigated, too, as you seek to bring your young people in touch with a children's theatre experience that will get them off to a good start.

The story of one successful group that very nearly missed its good start may serve to illustrate the point. The high-school theatre in Barrington, Illinois, has a twenty-year history of presenting theatre for children. The initial impetus came by way of seeing an excellent production of Charlotte Chorpenning's *The Emperor's New Clothes* performed at a National Thespian Society convention. Students who had seen it returned to their high school eager to share their enthusiasm with fellow students and to make plans for including children's theatre in the next year's production schedule.

The first step in stimulating interest seemed made to order when a professional touring company sponsored locally by the PTA came to perform for the elementary school children of Barrington. Excitement ran high as the high-school drama club anticipated a second exposure to the kind of theatre they had witnessed the summer before. But the performance was a disappointment. The company had prepared local schools with excellent publicity, but it was guilty of all the failures discussed earlier. If there had not been a prior exposure to something of good quality, that one experience probably would have killed any thought of a children's theatre in Barrington High School at that time. Because the group could turn to a happier memory of something well done, however, they reacted with "We can do better than that!"—and a new youth theatre for children was born.

Present Barrington High School actors and stage technicians continue in the tradition established twenty years ago. Many things have changed—a new theatre, audiences brought to it on school buses, a growing number of performances to reach a growing number of children—but the desire to bring something of value to a young audience remains constant. Barrington High School is pleased to be a part of a growing national movement, using the talent of the teen-agers to introduce good theatre into the lives of children.

Most youth theatres for children are organized within secondary schools and colleges as part of a varied theatre offering. Others are affiliated with community theatres, religious organizations, youth centers, libraries, and a variety of organizations featuring activities for young people. Whatever their sponsorship, most of them work closely with their local school administrators to define common goals and to set up a schedule that will be mutually acceptable.

Once you have stimulated interest among the young people who will work in your children's theatre, the next step should be to follow the course that has worked well for so many others and establish a working relationship with school authorities. This is a reasonable tie, since it benefits both. The children's theatre can provide a valuable learning experience that should please school officials, and working through the schools will give your theatre group a direct line of communication with the prospective audience.

If you are adding children's theatre to the activities of a high-school theatre, you can work directly with the high-school principal. When you have gained his interest, you can call upon him to contact the principals of elementary schools and develop a plan for bringing audience and performers together. Hopefully, that will mean a plan for bringing elementary school children to the high-school theatre during school hours or for touring the high-school players into elementary buildings to perform for assembled classes.

Of course, you cannot count on all administrators' realizing the values of a theatre experience, and you may have to prove your worth before you will be allowed to invade school time. If that is the case, the best arrangement you can hope for probably will be a plan for publicizing your venture as an out-of-school event. At least that will get your "foot in the door" and can provide the basis for more fruitful future dialogue with school officials.

Financial support may come in a variety of forms. Ideally, the program will be recognized as having as much educational merit as other learnings that are tax-supported and will be subsidized by the school system. Thus the theatre experience can be brought to all children, regardless of their ability to pay. Since both high-school and elementary-school pupils benefit, the cost may be shared by both. A more common practice, however, is for elementary schools to pay the children's theatre organization just as they might pay a professional group brought in to provide a program for a student assembly.

If financial support from the schools seems unlikely, perhaps the PTA or some other civic organization can be found with an interest in offering direct financial support in the form of a production budget, providing a block of tickets to be given to a selected age group, offering free admission to children who would otherwise be unable to attend, providing needed services such as transportation to performances, or supporting the cost of a publicity campaign.

You may even find that a working partnership with some other organization will serve your purpose well. That will mean a plan whereby a percentage of the play's income goes to the partner organization. Usually such an approach serves a temporary purpose, providing needed financial

backing until your own organization can function independently.

Once the business arrangements have been made, you can direct your attention to the happier task of getting ready for the first play production. Ideally two adults, a director and a technical director, provide professional leadership. Many children's theatres, however, function effectively under the direction of one adult. Teen-age ingenuity has no known limits, and by delegating responsibilities a director can spread his supervision pretty thin.

All committees and crews should function under youth leadership for maximum effectiveness. The value of the experience will be considerably reduced if anyone is made to feel that he is merely a part of the labor force for a theatre that really belongs to the director. Every member must know that it is *his* theatre and that others depend upon him to make it a good one.

We have come round to where we began these thoughts on starting a youth theatre for children. You and a group of young people, in an atmosphere of mutual respect, are about to share in a theatre experience that promises to be rewarding in many ways. Together you will select a suitable play, give it the kind of cast and committee leadership that can turn it into a successful, exciting theatre experience, and share in the pleasure of having made a significant contribution toward developing a young audience to its full creative potential.

So let's get on with the show! In coming chapters, we shall consider the play, the audience, the selection of a cast, the specific concerns of the actor and the director, the details of organization, the joys and problems of meeting your audience in your own theatre and on tour, and other thoughts relevant to the children's theatre experience.

Chapter II

THE RIGHT PLAY

Those who would write for children in any medium have a great responsibility and an exciting opportunity. It is exciting because it makes one a part of the discovery process that is the child's world. In that context, there is the evident responsibility of providing discovery experiences that are relevant to the life he is living and to the high hopes of our generation for his meaningful growth and development.

In the living theatre you are helping him to make his discoveries and form standards of taste and judgment in three-dimensional experiences, vastly more believable and more relevant to his real world than could be anything discovered on a television screen. You are, in fact, helping to counteract the influence of the flat world of TV by introducing the child to a more dynamic audience involvement with flesh-and-blood performers.

Consider the fact that a child feels very small in a very large world. Many things occur in his life to impress him with his smallness. There are obstacles he cannot overcome, powerful forces to which he must yield, and for some a sense of defeat that comes from failure to compete successfully with other children. Yet each child is capable of excited, imaginative involvement in experiences that deny his limitations. Each can find beauty and truth relevant to his world by reaching beyond it.

That is the challenge to playwrights and those who would perform for children. They must know children well enough to involve them in meaningful flights of imagination, revealing new insights into the nature of human relationships and carrying them beyond the experiences that could occur in the work-and-play activities of their daily lives.

To activate children's imaginations, the playwright must create characters with whom they can identify. Those characters must not be just small-size adults, expounding adult values on adult terms and sharing adult conflicts. Rather, they may well be grown-up versions of the children themselves. Empathizing with them, the children face and overcome a great obstacle, embrace a cause and realize something of the values for which they strive, make an exciting discovery and share in the new awareness it reveals, or simply share the sensory delights of soaring imaginatively into a dream world.

In all of this an important responsibility must be faced. One does not embark pointlessly upon "an adventure." The playwright and those who would do his play must ask: What kind of adventure? For what purpose? How does it relate to the child's knowledge, his experience, his dreams?

The great adventure of the real world the children face is the continuing need to adapt to change in a world of rapidly changing economic, social, and cultural patterns. Adventures shared in the theatre may be important schooling for the adventurous spirit required by the age in which they must be prepared to live.

Some children's entertainment, both on stage and in the mass media, has concerned itself primarily with "escape," concentrating on silliness, spectacle, or vigorous activity without purpose. Such theatre contributes little more than diversion for the children who share in it. Rapid change toward an unpredictable future with its resulting stresses may create a neurotic need for escape among adults who are ill prepared for it, but we can offer children something more than simply an opportunity to stop the world and get off.

It is not intended to suggest that the theatre experience be any less fun. But one can escape *to* rather than *from,* and that makes all the difference. Empathizing in the theatre, children make discoveries and are involved in conflicts that require them to make decisions. A playwright can involve them in decision-making that is relevant to their experience. He can provide discoveries that help to preserve fundamental truths that may seem obscure in the muddy waters of a changing society.

Or his adventure may breathe life into decisions and discoveries of the past that have relevance for the future. Professor Edward C. Cole of Yale University once referred to theatre as "the only means by which the living hand of the present generation can touch the living hand of past generations." Here the children of the present can recognize legendary names of yesterday as three-dimensional, living human beings whose meaningful experiences can be shared and used as a foundation on which to build purposefully for a better tomorrow. In the theatre they can feel aware of the roots from which they have grown and realize a sense of continuity that includes them in their own time. Those discoveries that have serious meaning and purpose are made more memorable by the fact that they have been realized through the fun and excitement of a theatre experience.

Much of the delight of children's theatre is found in fantasy, extending and expanding the world that is limited by reality. The lively imaginations of children reach easily in whatever direction the playwright may lead.

He has the opportunity to help children avoid the impression that the world is so mechanically ordered that dreams have no place in it. Children well schooled in fantasy will, in their teen years, find no need to escape conformity through "cool" detachment or lack of commitment. Apathy is an unlikely trait for one whose imagination can carry him beyond himself. Nor will he be overwhelmed by the daily discoveries of an evolving new world if he has long reached out to new worlds in fantasy.

Basic to all of this is an impression of life drawn from the playwright's unique insight. We look to the playwright for an awareness of truth in a changing world—not in pedantic or philosophical statements, but revealed through the adventures and discoveries of human beings, animals, and imagined creatures of whatever form. We look to the playwright for truths and values that are obscured in the struggle to keep pace with each day's needs as young people are tugged and torn by conflicting goals and the often confused or oversimplified definitions of good and bad offered by parents, teachers, preachers, police, big brothers, and Uncle What's-his-name on TV. We look to the playwright, too, to reveal his insights in a form that can excite fun and laughter, for surely children already have ample opportunity to approach learning in a climate of rigor and conformity.

The performing group may well employ more than one person in the task of evaluating a playwright's efforts and selecting a play for presentation in the children's theatre. Some directors prefer to assume full responsibility for choosing a play, but they would do well to consider the values gained by those performers and crew members who might share in the search.

Probably the most rewarding approach to the study of dramatic literature is the one that results in a meaningful theatre experience. That is the goal of those who read and analyze plays with a view toward ultimately selecting the one most suited to the talents of a performing group and the needs and interests of its audience. Meetings of such a group can be stimulating and exciting as

High-school students remembered this production of Greensleeves' Magic, *seen when they were third-graders, and campaigned vigorously for the opportunity to perform it. Their enthusiasm in-fluenced the decision, and* . . .

. . . this production was the result. Performers enjoyed knowing that the theatre excitement of their childhood had been repeated for a new generation.

plays are discussed and promoted or attacked on the basis of their suitability for the children's theatre production being planned.

The following list of criteria may serve as general guidelines for a play-selection committee. Detailed study of playwriting and dramatic criticism would be helpful, of course, but concern for the following practical considerations will help to avoid some of the pitfalls and go a long way toward helping a committee to make a wise choice.

1. *Characters worth doing.* Roles should be sufficiently well drawn so as to provide meaningful identification for the audience and something of a challenge for the performers.
2. *Theme worth expressing.* The playwright should reveal something better than a trite impression of life, significant enough to have lasting value for the audience and the players.
3. *Lines worth learning.* One way for a play to "go stale" in rehearsal is for actors to grow weary of the dialogue. Good literary quality helps to keep both the cast and the audience involved.
4. *Suitable cast size.* It would be impractical to consider a play calling for actors your group could not provide. A good selection should be made not only in terms of number, but also should give proper consideration to the interest, experience, and ability of those who will audition.
5. *Language and action suitable for children's theatre production.* The play should be readily understood by the audience for which it is intended. Avoid plays that involve "talky" scenes unless you know you can invent ways of bringing life into them. A good children's play should involve more *show* than *tell*.
6. *Suited to the audience age level.* Interests and tastes change as children grow older. You will want a play that has the power to attract and hold your particular audience. (This factor will be considered more fully in a later chapter.)
7. *Potential for interesting technical production.* The play should challenge the interests and abilities of your technical crews. Their imaginative efforts can be important factors in stimulating the imaginations of your audience.
8. *Helpful in generating an expanding interest in good theatre.* The play should extend and enrich the total theatre experience of both the audience and the performing group.
9. *Unlike other plays that have appeared recently in your theatre.* Variety is an important element in the long-range view of a theatre's program.
10. *Capable of effective production within the limitations of budget and facilities.* Consider carefully what you can afford and how much flexibility your stage will allow. Then select a good play that can be done well in your theatre.

Many of the plays most commonly found in the children's theatre are dramatizations of familiar children's stories. Rarely, however, does the playwright limit himself to the delineation of character presented by the original author. Nor is he limited by the theme, style, language, or even cast size of the original. Each work being considered must be judged on its merits as a play, not on the basis of previously held opinions of the original story.

Consider *The Sleeping Beauty,* for example, as it qualifies under the criteria cited earlier. It is, in its original form, a simple tale of proud parents, a beautiful child, a curse laid upon her, and the ultimate rescue by a handsome prince. The theme is obscure and there is little development of character motivation. In the hands of playwright Charlotte Chorpenning, however, it became a

Children learned that curiosity and ignorance were a dangerous combination . . .

. . . leading to an unpleasant surprise in The Sleeping Beauty.

believable theatre experience embracing a theme and having a beauty of its own.

The jealousy of the wicked fairy; the worry of the king and queen and their foolish decision to keep their daughter from ever seeing a spindle; her resulting curiosity the temptation to which she falls; the remorse of the king and queen as they realize their folly; and the joy of all as Beauty is restored by the act of a handsome prince: These motivations and actions offer something of substance for actors to work with and provide experiences that can bring excitement to the audience. Considering all the above factors, your group may well conclude that the play passes the first test of *characters worth doing.*

Mrs. Chorpenning has used the story to reveal how ignorance of danger can make that danger greater. Beauty might well have guarded against the promised threat of harm from a spindle if she had been permitted to know. With this *theme,* she may well be speaking to parents as well as children, and its meaning has value for any place or time.

The beauty of *lines* and the way in which she builds a variety of moods and responses assures the actors and their audience of another value. They offer a continuing challenge to the performers to improve upon their interpretation. Assuming that *cast size* is suitable for your group, those who perform will be provided a rich and varied experience.

Language and action, with all that has been said about the quality of dialogue, may still be a problem. Mrs. Chorpenning was an outstanding children's theatre playwright, but some of her scenes are quite "talky." That is especially true of the prince as he takes a rather long way to a decision before his rescue of Beauty. The problems imposed here should be considered carefully before deciding to produce the show.

Interesting technical production may be the factor that can save the "talky" scene. If talk is supported by something visually interesting, perhaps accompanied by interesting background sounds or music, it has a better chance of holding audience atten-

A most improbable flight to the moon revealed that it was peopled by equally improbable characters—each a unique challenge to the actors, the costumers, and the makeup artist—and creating a moonscape for The Man in the Moon *brought the imaginations of crew people into full play.*

tion and conveying its meaning. The problem will be considered in more detail in a later chapter.

Good technical production costs money, of course, and may require some special equipment as well as adequate space. Those considerations will affect your decision as to whether the play can be done *within the limitations of your budget and facilities.*

Considering *plays that have appeared recently in your theatre,* you may rule out *The Sleeping Beauty* because it follows too closely upon the production of another play adapted from a familiar children's story. You will turn then to one of the many fine originals that have appeared with increasing frequency in recent years.

Other factors on the list of criteria can be considered only after further review of your own theatre situation. *Knowing your audience* and analyzing the level of *interest in good theatre* within your performing group and in your community will help you to conclude that *The Sleeping Beauty* is or is not a good choice for you at the moment.

Whatever the decision, the people involved in making it have become caught up in the exciting responsibility cited at the beginning of this chapter. They have shared and, as the production continues, will continue to share in the process by which children make relevant discoveries and form standards of aesthetic judgment. It should not be at all surprising if, in this process, the young people producing the show make some discoveries and form some standards of their own.

Chapter III

KNOWING THE AUDIENCE

We live in a time of oversimplification, of easy generalization, of fixing labels and slogans, which seem to exclude the need for noticing differences. We are asked to buy a product, to oppose or embrace a cause, or to make a political decision on the basis of a catch phrase or word that, by connotation, seems to tell us *all* we need to know.

Those who would perform for children must guard against that fault of "allness" as they interpret the label, "Children's Theatre." It is too easy to say, "Kids will be kids," and accept a stereotype notion of little people who like a lot of noise and action, spiced by a bit of mischief. This judgment of the child audience results in a kind of theatre that demeans the child, talking down to him as one who is capable of no meaningful involvement and wants only diversion from the inhibited life pattern permitted by an adult-dominated society.

Certainly, the theatre offers the child a way of reaching through the walls of inhibition, but it can be something more relevant than noise and frenzy. It can be an invitation to stretch his imagination, reaching into the unknown past, reaching out to an unknown future, reaching toward the unknown thoughts and feelings of others, and reaching into his unknown self to discover truths that can give life a richer meaning.

Such discovery can begin with a theatre experience and can grow with the creative activity of children at play as well as in their private moments of fantasy and reverie. Psychologists have learned that much of the value of a theatre experience arises out of just such carry-over involvement.

A production should be planned, therefore, so as to open doors through which a child may pass in his imaginings, to provide the excitement, not of finding out how it ends, but of discovering how it all begins. The final scene is not "the end," but is a suggestion of how things will be from now on or what will happen next.

To have some assurance that suggestion in the theatre will result in that kind of discovery, the director, his cast, and his crew should have some awareness of the nature of their audience. The knowledge can be an important consideration in the selection of the play and certainly will influence the way in which it is presented. Regardless of the quality and kind of talent that actor and author bring to a theatre experience, it cannot produce a level of excitement or understanding beyond the audience's power to respond.

Three contributors are necessary to a meaningful theatre experience. Two of them, the player and playwright, contribute out of their own special talents; the audience contributes a response.

Before the days of TV-saturated youngsters, it was much more possible to estimate the degree to which a child of a given age had developed imagination and insight. Elements of surprise and excitement could be counted on to produce appropriate audience reaction. Now, however, all who write or perform for children must reckon with an unpredictable level of maturation and a new

A simple cutout was sufficient to represent a bird cage.

Children enjoyed the stimulus to imagination provided by the Oriental Property Man in The Land of the Dragon—*and, of course, scene changes were not difficult when they consisted of such devices as carrying on a branch to represent a forest.*

sophistication that confuse the issue of age in appraising the relevance of a theatre experience.

One result of reshuffling the maturation table—and perhaps the tendency of many parents to "push" their children too far too soon—is the appearance of much younger children in the theatre audience. Preschoolers, who ought to be busy discovering the world in which they live, too frequently are bypassing that stage of development and graduate from the two-dimensional make-believe world of television into the three-dimensional make-believe world of the theatre with something less than the level of readiness displayed by older children.

Even if one manages to perform for a largely school-age audience, the new sophistication encouraged by television, motion pictures, and comic books must be one of the factors that help to determine a kind of theatre that is currently relevant. What was moving or exciting in 1950 may be rejected as "corn-ball" now. Yet the need for a theatre that can excite a young audience now is as great as—or even greater than—it was in the 1950's. If that need is to be met, the nature of the theatre experience must be carefully analyzed. Any member of an audience can respond only in terms of what he knows and has experienced.

Consider, for example, the children of two divergent neighborhoods in a large city. In the first neighborhood they live in comfortable homes, feel secure in the love of their parents, travel at least once a year to a cottage or to some place of special interest, have pets to love and care for, and enjoy a variety of toys and games.

The second example involves children such as those who, when asked to identify a teddy bear on a standardized test, called it a rat because it was the fur-bearing animal they knew best. Their homes are uncomfortably crowded, and many of them find no joy in their contact with parents. They have only a vague awareness of things to do and places to go beyond the neighbor-hood and a nearby city park. They have no toys or pets.

The theatre experience will necessarily differ for those two audiences. The player and playwright may contribute the same talents, but the third ingredient cannot be the same. Sensitive to such differences, a performing group will seek to reach its audience in a manner that can produce a meaningful response.

One child's realism may be another child's fantasy. For some children, Dorothy's farm in Kansas may be just as remote as the mythical land of Oz to which she travels, and the first meeting with her dog Toto is potentially just as frightening as the initial impression of the Cowardly Lion. The implication here, of course, is that there is more than one way to do a scene. Knowing the audience will make it possible to anticipate the nature of audience response to a given moment in a play and to adjust the technique of performance so as to gain the most desirable response.

If you anticipate difficulty with vocabulary, you may find that unfamiliar language can have meaning when sufficiently reinforced by action. Or you may find it necessary to make minor adjustments in language to ensure clarity. Usually, however, well-motivated action will bring meaning to the words, and children will respond with a level of involvement and understanding that language alone could not have produced.

The most readily recognizable differences and the ones that you can act upon most easily are those of age. Actually the concern is for developing maturity rather than advancing age, and children do not all mature at the same rate. Here you face the same problem as do the schools in mapping out a curriculum.

Many schools now recognize that children do not all achieve readiness to approach new learnings at the same rate, and they are developing ungraded programs of instruction to permit children to advance at a rate consistent with their own advancing maturity. In the same sense, children do not all become adventurous at the same age, and their readiness for adventure in the theatre cannot be determined accurately by counting birthdays.

In a general way, however, some observations may be valid in considering the theatre readiness of children along the age/maturity lines designated as primary, intermediate, and upper levels in school. If audiences could be determined along those lines, the choice of appropriate theatre fare might involve careful consideration of their potential for effective involvement and response.

Primary children are just finding their way in the world beyond home, family, pets, and toys. They are living through an age of exploration and discovery, exercising a lively imagination to embellish the world around them with all sorts of fantasies. It is a time of intense involvement and belief in their discoveries, whether real or fanciful. They identify readily with the extremes of good and evil to be found in the familiar medieval storybook characters as well as in the ogres and witches of the old fairy tales.

Reward for good conduct and punishment of evil are very much a part of their own life experiences, and they readily accept them as appropriate behavior on the stage. Some care must be taken, however, so that actions are not too frightening for the more timorous members of the audience. Even though they may accept violence on the television screen, they are not necessarily ready for the same kind of thing in the more intimate three-dimensional presence of the stage.

Having little or no concept of history, primary children will accept "Once upon a time in a faraway place there lived a prince" as an adequate definition of time, setting, and character. But intermediate children have discovered that there is more of real life in the world than that which can be observed here and now. They are ready to go beyond the dream world of fantasy and to share the adventures of real people in real places. Although they may still find much to enjoy in fantasy, they probably are ready for more complex plots and can identify with characters having more complicated motivation.

They have learned enough of history and of legend to identify readily with characters who figured prominently in the adventurous past. They delight in stories of pioneer struggles against the elements in times and places that denied the use of modern conveniences, and heroic exploits in opposing the threatening forces of evil.

A play such as *Abe Lincoln—New Salem Days* has special interest because the children meet a man they already know and admire through their study of history, but during his formative years when they can more readily identify with him. Similarly, they enjoy reflecting on what they know of the tales of Charlemagne as they share in the adventures of his young nephew, Roland, in *The Magic Horn of Charlemagne*.

One need not, of course, limit the choice of plays to stories of the past with central characters drawn from the pages of history and legend. Such contemporary fictional plays as the Chinatown mystery *Little Lee Bobo* have great appeal. The magic word is *adventure,* whether historical, legendary, or fictional.

The upper level (middle school or junior high school) is the most difficult to plan for. Very few good plays have been written with the specific concerns of such audiences in mind. The reason may be that they are so filled with contradictions that the right approach is hard to find. They are growing through a time of deepening insight, but they are reluctant to let anyone know that they take themselves seriously. They are becoming capable of more complex emotions, but in the presence of their peers they will erase any show of sentiment with giggles and guffaws. This reaction can be disastrous in the theatre.

Plays are available, however, to which

Children were pleased to meet someone known to them through stories and the study of history in this production of Abe Lincoln—New Salem Days.

Designs for programs and posters meet the audience before the players do and can help prepare children for imaginative involvement.

Stories written for children are not beneath the entertainment level of adults. A good case in point is the musical Once Upon a Mattress, *based on the story "The Princess and the Pea."*

this audience will respond well. *Mrs. Mc-Thing* is a good example. When Mary Chase wrote it, she intended it as a play for children. In its professional runs, however, it turned out to be very popular with adults. It is a play for all ages beyond the primary level, but perhaps its greatest claim to glory should be that it plays well for the difficult age.

One important reason *Mrs. McThing* is successful with the preadolescent is its unique approach to telling a story. Intrigued by the fact that this is not another version of anything they have read or seen before, they become imaginatively involved—even to the point of sharing a sentimental moment without embarrassment.

Unfortunately, most of the things that purport to be aimed at this audience are hack-written and trite. They may get a few laughs, but they offer nothing to challenge the rich resource of imagination that this audience should be invited to exercise in the theatre.

One other approach may be worth considering. That is drawing upon another rich resource, the teen-age imagination. Members of your own group may have ideas for using innovative performance techniques or new dramatic forms that will appeal to the pre-high-school audience. One example of this approach was an unusual treatment given to the familiar *Alice* story and called *Alice in Retrospect*. It included original songs, absolutely wild technical effects, and a unique approach to dialogue—actors on stage performing in pantomime and synchronizing their lip movements with words spoken by amplified voices fed in from a battery of microphones on side stages. This and other creative approaches suited to the "middle-aged" audience are discussed in a later chapter on "Creative Play-making."

All attempts at classifying audiences assume that you will be able to perform for one level at a time. If that can be done there are, of course, some advantages. The practical fact is, however, that most audi-

ences are heterogeneous, and a good play must include various levels of appeal. Because children are perceptive and intent upon enjoying their moment in the theatre, they will find whatever the play offers on their own level and probably will reach beyond it. A good play performed well is likely to receive an appreciative audience response.

With all of our differences, we do have some important resources in common. Although the depth of our perceptions may differ, we all perceive with essentially the same kind of sensory equipment. Empathy, the remarkable feeling of identification with a character that occurs in the theatre, is communication between actor and audience requiring the active involvement of many senses. It is a shared awareness of tension, relaxation, heat, cold, pain, comfort, tastes, smells, sights, sounds, and all of the intricate combinations of sense experience to which one may respond with moods, attitudes, and emotions.

Primary children have been known to respond well to plays of Shakespeare, and adults have found much to involve them in *The Puppet Prince*. The differences lie in the depth of perception and the nature of the response. Primary children are likely to find their greatest involvement in action and visual details. (A play without exciting action and spectacle will very likely have them talking and running in the aisles.) Intermediate children are emotionally attuned to wants of characters. (Listen to them cheer at the moment of rescue.) Upper-grade children are intrigued by the process as well as the play. They may be lured by curiosity into coming backstage for an unscheduled tour.)

All children need experiences with good theatre—and they need *good* theatre more than they need an orderly progression from fantasy to adventure to more complex theatre experiences. The aim is to bring good theatre to children, not simply to bring a child audience to the theatre.

Chapter IV

WHO'S WHO

If you asked the man on the street to define *children's theatre,* he might be expected to say, "Children's theatre is a bunch of little kids putting on a play." He might make that assumption on the basis of having seen children involved in play-making activities—assuming that children's theatre is of, by, and for children.

He is quite right if we are talking about the kind of theatre experience that grows out of creative play or adult-directed activities in creative drama. That is the kind of acting that children should do as a fundamental part of their education. Volumes have been written on the nature and values of that kind of experience—but one important distinction must be made: It is not children's theatre, intended to involve an audience. It is creative drama, intended to involve the performers.

The best authorities in the field, speaking officially through the Children's Theatre Conference of the American Educational Theatre Association, advise that children should be over 10 years of age before participating as performers in a theatre experience. Until at least that age, they will gain more by being an audience in the formal theatre and a participant in creative drama.

Another source of talent for the children's theatre might be groups of parents. Certainly they have a good reason to be interested in providing a valuable experience for children. Many have tried, and some have, in fact, done some outstanding work as performers—but generally adults are too "set in their ways." The banker, the doctor's wife, or the shoe clerk has each developed a self-image out of countless interactions relevant to his life role. The well-worn paths of experience are comfortable and predictable, and many adults "feel foolish" if they step into new roles demanding new and different behaviors. Adults are accustomed to exercising authority over children, sometimes talking down to them. They have in their professional, vocational, and personal life roles developed inhibitions that are difficult to break through as they seek to identify with roles that can be meaningful to children.

If we rule out young children and most parents, that leaves the in-betweeners—the adolescent and young adult group. That has, in fact, been the greatest source of talent for the children's theatre. Outstanding work has been done in many universities, and a trend is rapidly growing to include children's theatre in the production schedules of high schools. Other groups sponsored by libraries, parks, churches, and youth organizations have been a part of the trend, too, and have turned their talents to the production of plays for children.

In our approach to casting, then, we will generally not look for little children to play children's roles and adults to play adult roles. We will rely on the versatility of young performers and the lively imaginations of children in the audience to maintain belief in a variety of characters.

Those who perform for children need some special qualities of animation and vocal versatility, and an ability to identify with

The script offers many clues to character that aid the actor in auditions and help guide the director to the wisest choice in casting. Care must be taken to make each a distinct personality when casting similar characters—like the deceitful cousins who care for Jade Pure in The Land of the Dragon.

the motivations of children. Those are the qualities that bring vitality and believability to the children's theatre.

The best way to cast a show is through some kind of audition procedure. It should be advertised by some means that will reach the people who will want to be involved. If the producing group is an organization that holds regular meetings or has a specified place where announcements are posted, there is no need for an elaborate campaign. If open auditions are the policy, however, a more general communication effort is required. Posters in school corridors, newspaper articles, and even announcements over local radio stations are appropriate means of spreading the word. Direct invitation is the most effective of all if there are people whose interest or talent has been recognized.

The use of an audition form calling for useful information about each applicant will speed up the audition process, provide useful information, and help to sharpen the director's memory of what has occurred during the tryout. If it carries a statement of the cast's commitment to a rehearsal schedule, it can serve as a kind of informal contract.

If the form contains space for listing all of the roles being tried for, it becomes a work sheet for the director during the audition. Having the applicant list roles in the order of preference provides one more bit of information that may be useful. Many things more important than the actor's preference are to be considered, of course, but if the director is faced with a toss-up decision as to which of two actors should be cast in a role or which of two roles an actor should fill, a stated preference may suggest something about the interest and enthusiasm that would be brought to the task of creating each character.

An audition may be organized in many effective ways. Perhaps the most common is to ask actors to read selected lines or scenes. They may be lines he selects and rehearses or they may be selected by the director and announced in time for actors to prepare.

One common practice is to have a first reading of a few speeches as an initial screening device. Then a second reading by those who are recalled can involve cooperative work on short scenes. The director is thus given a chance to observe character relationships as well as individual interpretation.

A second approach is the use of improvisation. It may be done in combination with the line-reading audition or as an alternative to it to avoid the error of judging someone entirely on his reading ability. Some good actors read mechanically and never really reveal their true potential until they have become free of the book.

Some directors prefer to abandon the book entirely in favor of unrelated audition material. They are looking for qualities demanded by the play, but they believe they can recognize those qualities better if actors are not hampered by their initial struggle to develop a concept of character and an interpretation of dialogue.

This approach calls for the use of nonsense materials (the alphabet, counting, etc.) with side coaching by the director. He may say, "Recite the nursery rhyme about Mary and her lamb—and you hate lambs. . . . Now try it again, only this time you are jealous of Mary." Or he may ask the actor to recite the alphabet, recognizing that each letter is a gift more valuable than the one before. With a little applied imagination, you can think of unlimited variations on this device for shaking an actor free of his inhibitions.

Side coaching is not necessarily limited to nonsense materials. Often the play and its characters will stimulate flights of imagination that suggest that the actor go beyond the realities of his prepared audition. When reading for *The Puppet Prince,* he might be asked to walk and perform various tasks as though his body were powered by a spring and all his movements mechanically pro-

The power of suggestion carries over to crew activities, too. A green beard and bean-shaped nose contributed an appearance to go with the name of Frihol in Jack and the Beanstalk.

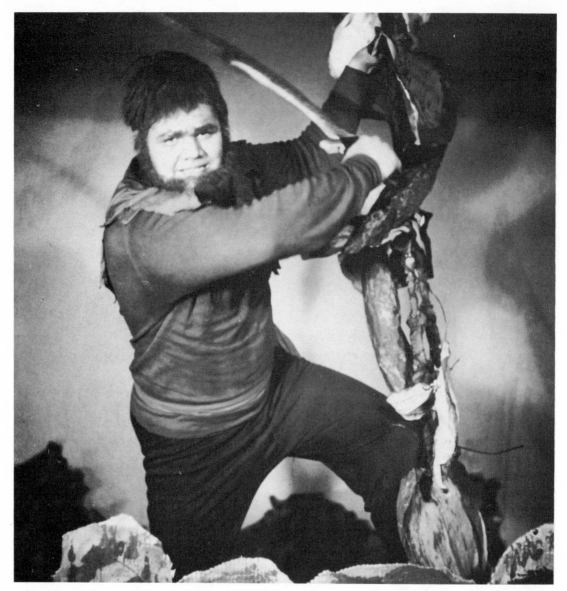

Some roles call for more than talent. For the Giant in Jack and the Beanstalk, *a big boy with a big voice was cast.*

grammed. Or for Frihol in *Jack and the Beanstalk* he might be told to walk and talk like a bean. There is, of course, no "right way" to respond to this kind of suggestion—but originality is called for and can produce some pleasant surprises.

Sometimes the name of a character can suggest a personality trait or some thoughts about his habits of speech and movement. What might we expect of a character called Fitzsneeze who appears in *Greensleeves' Magic*? Or of Angelica in *The Magic Horn*

of Charlemagne?

Auditions bring out a variety of psychological types, ranging all the way from the no-talent exhibitionist to the sensitive and shy person whose talent must be drawn out. There are those who prepare carefully and those who almost ask to be rejected by avoiding any preparation effort. The director's task is to see beneath the surface, hopefully discovering the true potential of the performer.

Nothing is gained by holding the reins so

tightly as to make the tryout a frightening experience. Sometimes an icebreaker in the form of informal conversation or a bit of humor is helpful. Or perhaps serious reading may be preceded by a nonsense exercise.

Generally, it is necessary for more than a single reading to be heard before the final cast is selected. One approach is to invite brief solo reading performances as a screening device. Then those who are serious contenders return for scenes in which two or three appear together after careful preparation. Some character analysis, orally or in writing, may be called for at this time as an additional aid to the director as well as a stimulus to the performer's imagination.

Whatever the approach to auditions, some important criteria are to be considered in making the selection. The most important measure of an actor's potential is his ability to communicate *belief*. He cannot *share* with an audience what he does not have. If he has belief in the essential truth that motivates the character and in the details of sensory experience to which the character must respond, his potential for effective performance is high.

Sensory awareness calls for use of another intangible, *imagination*. In experiences outside the theatre our senses reveal to our conscious minds the many details of an experience. Onstage the actor must not reveal to an audience those details that his senses record, but rather those details that his imagination creates. As *Rumpelstiltskin,* he may stand over a bubbling caldron. His own sense of sight tells him that a member of the stage crew is sitting in the caldron blowing bubbles, but his imagination must create a boiling brew and the red glow in his face must be realized as heat. Audition exercises calling for a response to such imaginings might be one way of revealing which actor is potentially best suited to the role.

Other criteria to be watched for are a flexible voice and an agile body. The actor must be able to move and speak in rhythms that belong to the life experience of his audience. Young children move readily from one extreme to another, from rest to leaping up, from joy to tears. As they grow older, their transitions from one mood or experience to another are less abrupt. The actor must be versatile enough in his use of voice and body to perform in the manner best suited to his audience.

In all of this there must be no pretense. Children are quick to identify the phony. They identify with the motivation for leaping away from danger or jumping for joy, not simply with the action. It is the ability to imagine and believe and respond truthfully in terms of the exaggerated rhythms of childhood that must be revealed in a successful audition.

Chapter V

CREATING BELIEVABLE CHARACTERS

Create is a powerful word. Or, rather, it suggests the active use of a unique power to produce something fresh and new. The theatre experience is a remarkable and complex adventure in creativity because it employs the creative power of so many people—all making unique contributions that must blend harmoniously if the artistic product is to be aesthetically pleasing.

The next four chapters will deal with the creative effort. To place the creative power of the actor in proper perspective, we must devote a moment here to an overview of the creative efforts that will be discussed more fully in the following chapters.

The initial creative spark comes from the *playwright.* His idea in literary form provides guidelines to direct and limit the efforts of those who design, direct, and perform. The *designer* works with colors, shapes, and textures to provide a visual effect that will best communicate the playwright's intention. The *director* creates believable events that can be arranged in the pattern provided by the playwright, and the materials with which he works are the various technical elements provided by designers and crew—and characters created by *actors.*

The characters think, feel, and behave in a manner consistent with the playwright's lines and they move according to the decision of the director, but they are given a foundation of truth and vitality because of the actor's creative effort. A worthy theatre experience results when, in the current jargon, each creator "does his thing."

To assure harmony in both the process and the product, it is important that each

contributor know the obligations he holds to the others and that each respect the others' efforts. The actor must know that the character—the child of his creative imagination—was born to be a part of events that are not his to design and control. He must accept direction and gratefully receive the benefits of scenery, properties, costumes, light, and sound provided by designers and technical crews.

To view the actor's effort quite literally, one must say that an actor does not "appear" in a play. The audience should not be aware of him any more than of the playwright, director, or designer. Only the created products *appear,* and they should blend unobtrusively into a theatre experience. Whenever any contributor seeks to call attention to himself or his work, the theatre experience is the less for it. Contrary to what one might think from reading the newspapers, the theatre is not a place for exhibitionists.

Truly, the actor is a contributor, not an exhibitor. But he cannot contribute without knowing what he has that can be given. "Know thyself" is a desirable directive to all people. For an actor it is more than desirable; it is an essential without which he is an unbelievable line-speaking machine.

Without concern for ego inflation, he must recognize that he has talent and find the means for employing it purposefully. Actor Joseph Jefferson once said, "Dramatic instinct is so implanted in humanity that it sometimes misleads us, fostering the idea that because we have the natural talent within, we are equally endowed with the power of bringing it out." Having "the natural talent within" should not be a cause for hyper-ego if, indeed, it is "implanted in humanity." Rather, it is the basis for an actor's feeling of "oneness" with all fellow humans.

The actor is seeking the creative "power of bringing it out" so that he can use this common property of all humanity as a beam on which to communicate human experience. In a word, he is seeking *truth* to be used as a solid foundation on which to build *believable* experiences—whether they take the recognizable form of reality or the distortion of fantasy.

Most of what can be said to instruct an actor in the children's theatre applies equally well to a good actor in any play for any audience. *Truth* is a universal quality and must provide the foundation for an artist's work in any medium. It is the most significant factor in discerning the difference between artistry and display.

Previous chapters have established the need for quality and value in the children's theatre experience. If the actor is to contribute effectively toward the performance of a play that deserves an excited audience response, he must approach his creative task with the same depth of involvement that he would give to any other role.

Depth is achieved by digging. The actor must dig into himself to find the motivations to serve his character. If the character knows fear or joy or sorrow, the actor must draw upon his own experience to realize the powerful feelings demanded by the role.

But how does one tap those resources? What happens when powerful feelings are stirred? Can one really feel anger or excitement by making the effort to *dig* them out of his own experience?

Addressing himself to the problem, Edward Goodman said, "If at first you don't succeed, *don't try* again." [1] By this he did not mean to suggest that the actor should

---

[1] Edward Goodman, *Make Believe: The Art of Acting,* Charles Scribner's Sons, 1956, p. 62.

quit after his first unsuccessful attempt. He meant, rather, that an essential part of the actor's "digging" is effortlessness. His digging tool is concentration, and one cannot concentrate while feeling the strain produced by conscious effort. He must free his mind of everything but the *sensory* details of an experience involving the desired emotional response.

It is the process that occurs in dreams—and in daydreams. Without the presence of physical stimuli, the dreamer creates an awareness of sensory details and responds to them emotionally. Even body chemistry is affected as though the experience were real. Concentration on an experience involving danger and a need to escape will cause the adrenal glands to function and the heartbeat to accelerate just as they do in dreams.

In that way the actor can overcome self-consciousness in preparing his character to do things he himself would never do. He might "feel foolish" making the effort to produce the behavioral extremes called for by a role, but through concentration he can reach through the wall of inhibition to touch hands with the past and lead it effortlessly through to the surface of his current awareness.

Reached for in that way, his fear or joy becomes *believable*—a rich resource to be used by the character and shared with the audience. By such use of his "talent" he causes his audience to share his dream, now translated into a new situation called for by the playwright. That sense of sharing is the dynamic essence of the theatre experience.

To understand how the technique of reaching for truth works, one must recognize that emotion can be practically defined only in terms of response to sensory stimuli. Love, fear, hate, joy cannot exist except as they are prompted by some sensory experience. One could not feel love for his mother if he never had known her physical presence, or know fear of a weapon if his senses had not associated it with danger. To have "feelings" about someone or something, one must see, hear, taste, smell, touch, or realize in terms of movement, muscle tension, temperature change, pain, or organic sensation. Generally an emotion is generated in response to some combination of the senses as they communicate the realities of experience.

Imagination is a means of "turning on" patterns of awareness without having the realities present to produce the stimuli. By imagining his way back into some past reality, the poet is stimulated to write, the artist to paint, the actor to act. Imagination produces the materials out of which each can *create*. Each in his own medium deals with elements of *truth* drawn out of himself and produces something original in a form that can be communicated to an audience.

That kind of imagining is freely employed by children, with little or no distinction made between fantasy and reality. In the child's world, truth is truth, whether it is in response to realities or imaginings. He has not yet learned the inhibitions that limit adult behavior and is free to respond honestly and openly. He is thus wonderfully responsive to the actor who is similarly honest in sharing something of himself through the character he has created.

The fundamental nature of inner truth makes it possible for an actor to find in himself the foundation for characters quite unlike himself. To play the witch in *The Tinder Box*, for example, the performer must demonstrate an overwhelming self-interest and produce outbursts of rage when things do not go her way. Like Rumpelstiltskin, she delights in her scheming but cannot tolerate defeat.

It would be difficult to find a good actress who could draw those qualities out of her own normal attitudes and behavior. Indeed, it would serve no worthy purpose. Yet by reaching far enough into her past, a good actress can find childhood experiences in which the extreme frustration of not getting her own way spilled over as tears or a temper tantrum or a burst of energy directed against something or someone. Remembering how she felt when she kicked a chair or smashed a toy in anger will help give power to the line in which she rages after a fall, "You rotten rope! I'll have you knotted until you're just one bunched-up bundle of bumps!"

One word of caution is necessary here. The use of an actor's emotional resources in creating a character is *not* another way of saying that he "loses himself" in the role. That implies a loss of control, something an actor must never permit to happen in performance. He does not *lose* himself; rather, he *uses* himself. The powerful resources are within him and must come to the surface for use, but they do not take over. Establishing such control over a powerful and volatile resource is one of the purposes of rehearsal.

Beyond the essential reaching into oneself is the matter of creating the externals of the character. That involves a search for clues in the script. What has the playwright said to describe size, posture, movement, voice, etc.? Are there clues to character in the descriptive details? And what's in a name? Does a name like *Angelica* or *Adora* provide some hint of the playwright's intention?

In *Greensleeves' Magic* the playwright describes a character as "a haughty, disdainful fellow with his nose always high in the air. He constantly peers down it as he speaks to lesser mortals." Add to that description a name like *Fitzsneeze* and you have many clues to stir your imagination before reading a line of dialogue.

Looking further, what does the dialogue reveal? If someone is frightened by a character's stern look or impressed by his regal bearing or amused by his funny beard, the actor must create the kind of character who can call forth those reactions.

To do so, he will find it helpful to observe life beyond his own experience. To create a character, he may want to draw bits and pieces from many varied observations. From one person he may borrow a speech mannerism, from another a tilt of the head or a way of walking or a kind of posture that seems to imply an attitude toward those around him.

Even animals and inanimate objects can suggest useful character traits. Have you ever heard an angry voice with the harsh incisive quality of a buzz saw or one that suggested the incessant cackling of a hen? Descriptive similes or metaphors invite the actor to make some useful observations that can add to the store of materials from which he will build a character.

In *The Tinder Box* is a character called the High Cockalorum who fancies that his crowing and strutting cause the sun to rise each morning. To prepare for that role, an actor might well spend some time in a farmyard watching and listening. A lot of "people" worth studying can be found on farms and in zoos if you add the humanizing element of imagination.

When observing, the actor must be careful to look for the *why* of observed behaviors. If he is observing the pretentious posturings of a peacock or the anxious cackling of a hen or the pitiable sadness on the face of a cocker spaniel, the *why's* must be imagined as meaningful human motivation. Observations of people, of course, involve a search for the real reason behind the thing observed.

Whatever he finds useful in the creating of his own character must be adapted as *honestly motivated* behavior. To observe purposefully, therefore, he should *empathize* —reaching into himself for an awareness of the sensory activity that produces the observable response. To observe properly the behavior of an injured man limping, for example, one must realize the pain that limits the amount of weight a knee or ankle can accept. Then, in adapting the observation to his performance, he trusts the motivation to produce the effect. Thus imitation can be made believable.

Strong feelings expressed in the children's theatre are based on the same fundamental truths as for the more mature adult emotions. Children respond to an awareness of love in this scene from Ali Baba and the Forty Thieves.

The actor in a children's theatre production has a further challenge beyond that of theatre for adults. Because he is playing for an audience of young people, he must make his character's behavior meaningful in their terms. That means *extending responses* to stimuli beyond the restrained behaviors that characterize adult responses.

A child is much more likely to give overt physical expression to his feelings—laughing, shouting, and leaping in a moment of joy that might cause an adult to smile, speak brightly, and quicken his step.

The enlarged physical response typical of performance for children is good experience for actors —discovering fully the responses that are played with greater restraint in theatre for adults. Total involvement is apparent in this picture of a troubled Ali Baba in Ali Baba and the Forty Thieves.

The honesty with which a child responds to truth—whether in real or imagined experience—has made it possible for relatively untrained child actors to "steal the show" from experienced adult professionals. That same honesty plus something like a child's exaggerated energy are essential ingredients in the performance of anyone who creates a character with which a child is expected to identify.

The energetic quality of performance in the children's theatre is no more than an extension of the responses that might be appropriate for a more mature audience. *It is not pretense.* Action must be motivated, not just "thrown in" to excite the audience. That is a vital distinction if the children's theatre performer is to be more than a "ham actor."

With believable characters performed in a style that transcends reality, actors of any age can communicate honestly with their child audience.

Chapter VI

CREATING BELIEVABLE EVENTS

The essential element an actor contributes to a play is a believable character. That character, then, becomes one of the materials with which a director works in rehearsal as the entire production team seeks to evolve *believable events*. Those happenings are given purpose and significance by the manner in which they develop under the guiding hand of a director.

Because his guiding hand often must extend itself to pointing the way for actors to learn the fundamentals of their art, the danger is always present that the busy director will make it *his* business to create the characters and invite his actors to be imitators. He must frequently remind himself that teaching actors to act does *not* involve dictating the interpretation of a line. More specifically, it does not involve getting up onstage to *show* the actor how it is done.

Much of the truth and vitality disappear from an actor's performance if he is an imitator. The director must have the patience to watch and wait as the character evolves out of the actor's creative effort.

I do not mean to suggest that the director has no influence on what the actor does. The actor must rely on him for *direction*. When he is lost, as he very likely will be at times during the early stages of rehearsal, the director points the way—or, rather, helps him to *find* the way.

One of the most important functions of the director is to be a *reactor*. He reacts to the characters as they interact, then raises leading questions or offers constructive criticism of those moments that he cannot *believe* or that are not in *harmony* with the

style of the production. When he feels comfortably involved, *reacting as he would want his audience to react,* he knows that the scene has grown as much as it can under his direction.

Before he can be that comfortable with a production, he has a long, hard road to follow. Basic decisions about style and period must be made early and communicated to all who contribute to the total creative effort. The decisions should be the product of whatever research is necessary and full discussion of ideas and plans with all heads of committees and crews. Involving others in the thinking that leads to decision will ensure mutual understanding and a unified production effort.

The first concern that must be discussed with actors, designers, and technicians in every phase of production is the nature of the child audience for which the play is intended. Subtleties of movement, interpretation, and decor, which may combine artfully to please an adult audience, may be lost on an audience of children. Everyone must understand them as well as he understands the skills that are his special contribution. That understanding is the key to *style* in the children's theatre.

The play emerges by an evolutionary process called *rehearsal*. In the beginning, nobody looks good. The director can be much more patient with the slow growth toward excellence if he realizes that the only positive quality revealed in early rehearsals is *potential*.

The director will help that potential to be realized if he approaches rehearsal with an optimistic spirit, a plan establishing goals and deadlines, and a continuing patience. The director who spends his time complaining of the actors' inadequacy and the slow progress of the crew, or who "blows his top" when all does not go well, satisfies himself that he is doing something about his problems—but, really, he interferes with the creative evolution of the play.

An orderly approach to rehearsal calls for the publication of a schedule, indicating exactly which scenes will be rehearsed at each anticipated rehearsal and setting deadlines for the activities of various committees and crews. A schedule of that kind, if it is followed carefully, offers advantages to all concerned.

The schedule aids the director by prodding him to move on when he might be tempted to spend more time on early scenes, striving for excellence on things begun before getting on with new material. Perhaps you have seen plays that started well but seemed to have last acts that were not quite ready to meet their audience. That is the inevitable result when the director believes that one scene should be polished before the next is begun. Time runs out and the final scenes, perhaps potentially the brightest gems of all, are left to be shown in the rough.

The actor finds a schedule important because it clearly indicates when scenes must be memorized, which rehearsals will require his attendance, and when he will have time free. It helps him to avoid those awkward situations when he has promised to be in two places at once as well as the frustration of attending a rehearsal of scenes in which he does not appear.

Committees and crews holding to a schedule can avoid those unpleasant moments when a cast must attempt to dress-rehearse with the noise of hammers in the background as crew heads face the awful truth that two weeks' work must be done in three days. In fact, if they approach final technical and dress rehearsals with a terrible sense of urgency, they cannot properly view their place in creating a believable climate in which believable events can be revealed onstage.

The purpose of the first rehearsal is to discover the play. In a second meeting specific action is introduced. Then the cast works to develop *habits* of speech and movement consistent with the characters involved and capable of serving the playwright's intention. Finally, all is transplanted into a completed stage setting and rehearsed with the stage crew so that all can function comfortably, believing in the place and the characters they have created.

The amount of time required to accomplish the finished product will vary with the producing group, depending largely upon available time. The schedule in Appendix D suggests a six-week period for both cast and crews. The first three weeks are given to developing basic habits of speech and movement; the fourth week is for reinforcement of those habits and developing a deeper awareness of character motivation; the fifth week adds the suggestive power of scenery, lighting, and special effects; and the sixth week is for technical and dress rehearsals, polishing every detail except the unpredictable element of audience response.

The schedule cited assumes that four nights a week are available for rehearsal. Many varying approaches to the use of that time are possible, of course, even though the general objectives mentioned here remain the same.

The objective of the first rehearsal was said to be discovering the play. The means of making that discovery will vary with the differing approaches to the first rehearsal made by various directors.

Most directors will invite actors to work with manuscripts, either improvising action or reading in character while seated informally. With no special concern for being in the right place at the right time, they are free to involve themselves completely in the developing story. In the reading, imagination should reach far beyond reality into the extremes of a child's world of fantasy. Voices should play on those extremes, and muscles should tense in response to the motivations that call for movement. The aim from the very first is *belief*. And with belief comes the discovery that *the play is not in a book but in an experience being shared.*

Some directors prefer to make that point more directly by not permitting the use of a book at the beginning. Their approach involves discussion of the characters and the playwright's purpose as well as consideration of whatever they can learn about the audience. Then, guided only by a scenario or a verbal description of each event, they improvise the play—working toward the script rather than from it. Through improvisation and discussion the play evolves out of group creative activity, and the lines composed by the playwright ultimately are accepted as a means of expressing relationships and attitudes that already have become quite believable.

Whether by improvisation or by early memorization, the cast should be free of handling books during most of the rehearsals. One way to accomplish that is to drop scripts on about one third of the play after each of the first three weeks.

To avoid mechanical memorization by rote, dialogue should be learned as a part of—not apart from—the action of the play. *Memorize on your feet* is good advice. Action keeps the lines in context and shortens the time it takes to master them.

During the same three-week period, actors come to know one another in character and become familiar with the situations in which they interact. To aid in the development of necessary thoughts, feelings, and insights, the director should interrupt frequently to raise questions or invite discussion of motivation or character relationship. As believable responses are developed, they must be enlarged to a style of performance appropriate to the play and to the age level of the child audience.

After the fourth week there should be no more interruptions of scenes in rehearsal, permitting a deeper level of concentration and a feeling of continuity for both the players and the director. That makes it possible for them to realize more fully the experiences they share and to which they must respond with belief.

At that point and until the final rehearsal, the director carries a clipboard to make notes or dictates to an assistant whenever anything interferes with his *belief* in the events unfolding onstage. Those notes, if made on a separate sheet for each performer, may be studied before the next rehearsal. Or the director may prefer to confer with each actor to be sure that his suggestions are clearly understood.

The final two weeks are the period of maximum growth. As the play develops, each event should *feel* as though it has grown out of what has gone before, and each rehearsal should be more exciting and believable. The exaggerated movement that helps a young audience to become involved can have an exhilarating effect on the actor as well. His body moves, and his mind and spirit respond—and those thoughts and feelings motivate still more physical reaction as total involvement creates a believable event.

During dress rehearsals, it is the director's business to play the role of audience for each actor, identifying with his character and realizing the audience involvement that is stimulated by the performance. This really is fun time for the director because, if the play is going well, he is thoroughly entertained. His concentration on belief in sensory-emotional detail during earlier rehearsals has paid off and he finds that the playwright's words have come to life and he can respond with appropriate excitement.

Because the performance will require a high level of energy and concentration, a night of rest between the final dress rehearsal and the opening performance usually will be of greater value than any additional work that might be done. Just knowing that there is time for rest helps to build confidence, too, and the actor has time to realize that he has created something of value, which he can look eagerly forward to sharing.

If rehearsals are to follow the procedures and accomplish the goals that have been generally outlined here, the director must do his homework before rehearsals begin. He must analyze the play and the audience and devise means whereby the two may be brought together in a common experience. He must identify intellectually with the playwright as he seeks to understand what he has intended to communicate, and he must identify emotionally with the characters as he seeks to know their motivations and to realize the responses he will expect from the audience with whom the play ultimately will be shared. Then he must note carefully the details of stage movement that will help to transform the actors' lines into believable events, consistent with the playwright's intention.

Usually the script will contain a suggested floor plan for each scene and may include photographs from some previous production.

The director is not obliged to follow the publisher's suggestions but probably will find them helpful as he and the technical crew determine the best plan for creating a workable design to be used on their own stage. Basic floor plans including door and window openings, location of major properties, and the size and shape of various levels must be completed for the director to use before rehearsals begin.

With a sketch of the floor plan or a model of the set before him, he should set up tentative patterns of stage movement before he calls a blocking rehearsal on each act. The plans are tentative because they ought to change as actors in rehearsal evolve motivation for added movement. They are an important first step, however, because they help actors to avoid the natural inclination to stand and talk a scene rather than act it, and they provide a shortcut to the finalized movement that will belong to the characters just as surely as does the dialogue.

Some directors like to work with small pieces of wood or paper or with doll figures identified as the characters appearing in a scene. That keeps the visual image of the scene constantly in view as actions are

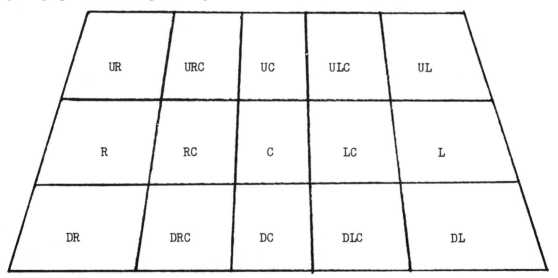

UR	URC	UC	ULC	UL
R	RC	C	LC	L
DR	DRC	DC	DLC	DL

The above diagram indicates upstage (U), downstage (D), right (R), left (L), and center (C) locations, and their abbreviations are used in combination to indicate fifteen general areas of the stage where actors may be asked to move and where stage properties or scenic elements may be situated. If all cast and crew members understand these area designations, both oral and written communication can be simplified and improved.

planned. Others prefer to make a succession of pencil sketches representing changes in the stage picture that develop through movement.

Whatever the method, the director must consider the basic principles of composition so as to maintain a pleasing stage picture. Unlike a static composition, however, the picture is constantly in motion, and the focus of attention shifts from one person or object to another. No one should be moved or placed in a scene so as to detract from the focus that will best serve the playwright's intention at any given moment.

Usually some stage directions are suggested by the playwright in his published manuscript. They may be based on his ideas of how the action should be directed or on what developed in the first production of the play. Sometimes those suggestions are very helpful, but often they will be inconsistent with your concept of the stage settings, your facilities for staging, or your actors' interpretations of the roles. Almost always the director will find it necessary to add substantially to the suggested directions.

Marginal notations of the directions should be made by the actors and followed carefully in early rehearsals. The notes should always be made in pencil, however, to permit changes as the play develops, and abbreviations should be used for speed in note-taking and for ease in following directions.

Finding means of focusing and shifting audience attention is one of the director's continuing concerns as he blocks patterns of action. Of primary importance here is the principle, *attention follows movement*. Audience interest can be directed immediately to any place on the stage where action occurs. In the children's theatre that often means lively action—extending the subtleties of adult response into something paralleling the exaggerated quality of child behavior.

The principle of attention-getting must be carefully considered because it can serve the play for both good and ill. A time-honored misuse of the principle is *scene-stealing*. It occurs when an actor, whether accidentally or intentionally, calls attention to himself through movement when the purpose of a scene is best served through directing attention elsewhere. The animated behavior of characters in a children's play will be distracting unless they move toward or are reactions to whatever occurs in the area that should hold audience attention.

A second consideration that guides the director in his decisions as he blocks movement is the psychological value of actor placement in a scene. The changing composition of a stage picture allows for a constant shifting in positions of relative strength and weakness among the characters. The dialogue provides clues to the changes, but it is up to the director to present them visually as a means of reinforcing what language can suggest. Words alone could not create the kind of excitement that is characteristic of good children's theatre.

Four factors contribute to relative strength and weakness as characters interact. They are location, level, profile, and action. The *location* on stage that gives the greatest feeling of strength is upstage center (UC) because a person in that position can relate effectively with all other characters while facing the audience, and they must turn away from the audience to give attention to him. Similarly, a character gains strength over another anywhere on the stage by moving to a position upstage of him.

Any character who stands taller than another, assuming comparable stage location, profile, and action, gains strength over him. That kind of relationship may be accomplished in many ways: One may stand while another kneels or is seated; one may sit tall while another slumps; one may be on a step, platform, wall, rock, or tree stump while another is on the level of the stage floor. The foregoing suggests the value of designing a variety of *levels* into the scene, making it possible not only to maneuver characters in

A part of the director's job is to see that characters move in ways that call attention to the center of interest in a scene. In this scene from Tom Sawyer, *Tom gained strength by moving downstage as the Minister, Aunt Polly, and Sid turned toward him.*

terms of location onstage but to consider elevation as well.

Wherever a character is situated and at whatever level, he gains strength as he moves closer to facing downstage (D). Two characters standing on the same level and in comparable stage locations are equally strong in the scene as long as they maintain the same *profile*, but a simple turn can change their relative strengths.

Although *action* of any kind attracts audience attention, moving downstage adds strength. If, in addition, other characters react by moving out of the way, back away before the advancing figure, or turn in weak profile, his strength is made greater still.

Another factor that may or may not be related to the comparative strength of characters is *focus*. Unlike motion pictures or television in which there is a choice of camera angles to present and the capability of zooming in for a close-up, live theatre must depend upon the placement of characters and variations in stage lighting to give emphasis to a particular place on the stage. The most obvious way is to have all other characters onstage turn to face the one who commands attention. He may be emphasized further by having him stand framed in an arch or doorway.

Placing a character in a position that sharply contrasts with that of others on the stage also draws attention his way. He may be the only one moving or the only one still while others are moving. Or he may be seated while others stand, or vice versa. The setting and the spirit of the play will stimulate the director's imagination to consider other ways in which appropriate contrasts may be set up so as to focus attention on the character he wishes to emphasize.

Of primary importance in the blocking of a scene is *motivation*. In his concern for creating a pleasing stage picture and considering problems of balance, strength, and focus, the director must be continually aware of the *character's reasons for movement*. At no time is it possible to move a character only to achieve balance or focus. Those are directors' motives and should not be on the actor's mind. The actor must concern himself entirely with the character's thoughts and feelings.

Motivation complicates the director's task in preparing for a blocking rehearsal. If he is to work effectively with actors in creating believable events, he must empathize with each character as he considers movement that is in harmony with the dialogue. When he directs an actor to leap up on a tree stump or move to an upstage position, he must know that the character will *feel* like leaping or moving away.

As rehearsals progress beyond the initial blocking of movement, it is quite likely that some of the action will be found inadequate as originally planned. Characters eventually will *know* what they must do, and their feeling of involvement will go beyond the educated guessing of the director.

If he has identified well with character mo-tivation in his prerehearsal planning, changes probably will be a part of growth and development and will not produce conflicting ideas. It is possible, however, that an actor occasionally will find it impossible to accept directed action because it is not in harmony with his concept of the role.

When such a conflict arises, the director gains nothing by asserting his authority and dictating a decision. It must be resolved through a mutual understanding of the character's function in the scene. Dictated action is unmotivated action, and the play is made less believable as a result.

If both actors and directors recognize that beneath the surface of exaggerated onstage behaviors there must be a core of truth—no less valid than the truths that govern behavior in life itself—the rehearsal period will be a time of working creatively together; and the result will be a viable and exciting theatre experience for the performers and audience and for the director as well.

Chapter VII

CREATIVE TEAMWORK

The kind of harmony that characterizes the working relationship of actors and director must extend to all facets of production if a play is to achieve unity of purpose. Theatre is a group art, and all who participate in it must recognize their dependence on one another—encouraging and appreciating rather than demanding and criticizing as they work together toward a common goal.

The amateur theatre would do well to avoid calling anyone "the lead" or "the star," and in the children's theatre such a designation betrays misunderstanding of the child audience and the purpose of the theatre experience. To paraphrase Mr. Shakespeare, *the play's the thing* wherein we'll catch the imaginations of children. Any special attention given to one person's contribution detracts from the goal of a *shared experience* and tends to minimize the importance of many who do not find their way to the spotlight but without whom no "star" could shine.

Quite as important as the actors are those who design settings, plan lighting, build scenery, build and gather stage properties, design and make costumes, and provide special effects such as musical background, sound effects, and puffs of smoke. Like the actors, each makes a contribution that would be meaningless in itself but that becomes a part of the whole. Emerson might well have had the children's theatre in mind when he wrote:

All are needed by each one;
Nothing is fair or good alone.

Each person who contributes to any part of the show should feel an aesthetic involvement in it. To the extent that anyone considers himself to be a performer or master of tasks rather than a significant contributor to a creative group effort, the level of artistry will be reduced. Every idea should be heard, and every effort should be acknowledged through a spirit of mutual appreciation. When the audience says, "Thank you," with its applause, the thrill of success should be felt no less behind the scenes than onstage where the bows are taken.

The key to that kind of spirit is *involvement*. The director and technical director are guides, aides, catalysts, active supervisors—but not dictators. "Because I said so," is never a satisfactory answer to a question, and it is particularly unsatisfactory in any kind of creative effort. *The best leaders are the best listeners* in any kind of human endeavor; in the group art of theatre, a poor listener is clearly a liability.

That prefatory comment seems necessary to a discussion that is largely task-oriented. The fact is that many of the most creative people in the theatre get their hands dirty and work hard to the point of weariness. Mounting scenery, hanging lights, carrying heavy props, and rigging sound effects are means to an end. The artistic product cannot be realized without them.

The behind-the-scenes effort begins with a scene design, and the design begins with an idea. The idea is a concept that develops in the minds of the director and technical artists for the most appropriate execution

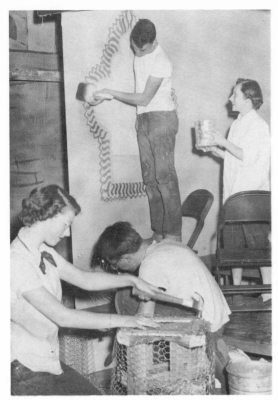

A stage carpenter is not necessarily male. Boys and girls share the many tasks that combine to bring a scene designer's idea to the stage.

of a playwright's work. The idea or concept need have no limitations; it is as free and expansive as a dream. The scene design is a compromise between the idea and the physical limitations and resources of the stage.

The design for *Greensleeves' Magic* was developed through the efforts of a scene design class and began with a number of crude pencil sketches inspired by a reading of the play. These were circulated through the class, and anything that seemed an interesting and stage-worthy visual effect was circled. Further screenings produced a combination of scenic elements to be used, and ultimately one person's rendering of a complete design was selected.

Another approach to selecting a design might be to have several people work independently to prepare color sketches or stage models. The thought process would be the same, working from the play to an idea to a scene concept, but each designer would

work alone until ready to submit tangible results to the director and technical director for consideration.

In any case, the scene designer approaches the production from two points of view. First, he must design his setting to perform the basic functions required by the script and the director's concept. There must be openings, levels, and other scenic elements placed on the stage in such a way that the actors can perform the actions called for. Second, he determines how those elements may be treated so that their line, proportion, and color contribute effectively to the total production.

To do so, he must understand his audience and plan for the kind of technical detail that will enhance meaning and produce a proper climate for an exciting theatre experience on their level. His imagination must keep pace with that of children who, as they have read the descriptive detail in stories, have imagined many scene designs of their own.

Children coming to the theatre expect to see the pictures they have created in their minds equaled or surpassed as people and places achieve three-dimensional reality onstage. That does not mean settings must be complete to the last detail or done in naturalistic style. Quite the contrary is true, as the lively imaginations that serve children so well as they read or listen to a storyteller are even more stimulated in the theatre. Design should be colorful and style consistent, but a strong element of suggestion is more important than a meticulous concern for detail.

If your theatre reaches an audience of preschool children, most published plays of an hour or more in playing time are inappropriate. A limited attention span suggests the possibility of several short items on a program with colorful costumes, properties of exaggerated proportion, and brightly painted screens, blocks, or boxes used to provide scenic suggestion. Small children are likely to be overwhelmed by an elaborate production in a large theatre and will re-

This setting was a composite of many designs submitted by students in a high-school class. The best elements of each were brought to the stage for a production of Greensleeves' Magic.

spond more favorably to simple scenic elements and/or a puppet theatre presented in a space that permits a close rapport between the audience and the center of interest.

The greater sophistication of the primary-grade audience makes them responsive to colorful spectacle and fanciful design. Because of their school experience as well as their greater exposure to stories, films, and television, they are ready to enter a theatre with a larger audience and share in the excitement of stimulating visual images.

Belief in the theatre at any level is more closely related to things seen than things heard. That is especially true for children in the primary grades, in whom limited language comprehension may cause spoken dialogue to produce a response more by its mood and melody than by its meaning. Under those conditions the technical crews speak eloquently to their audience as they display the fantastic land of Oz or transform the dismal palace grounds into a wonderful "secret place" through the magic of Greensleeves or reveal the place just upstage of a scrim-paneled forest where Beauty lies sleeping.

Perhaps *scrim* is a word that needs explanation. It is a product that serves the children's theatre well. Scrim is a loose-woven fabric that can be seen through readily when light is directed on anything placed behind it. But when light comes from any source above, below, or beside it on the audience side, the threads cast shadows against each other and make the surface appear to be solid. It can be dyed or painted to look like other flat surfaces in the setting, creating the illusion of a solid wall until a change of light causes it to melt away and reveal a wicked witch, a pumpkin coach, or a sleeping Beauty. Although special products sold as sharkstooth scrim and theatrical gauze by theatre supply houses will serve best, other transparent fabrics such as tarlatan and cheesecloth have been used successfully.

Such devices may also be used in more adventurous plays for children of the intermediate grades, but they prefer to view them as magic or have them frankly acknowledged as stagecraft. They prefer visual effects that have some relevance to the world they live in or have visited through books, and they enjoy techniques that spark their curiosity. They are interested in being transported out of the here and now, but they are equally interested in knowing how they got there.

Because they are intrigued by the realities of stage production, they are likely to be filled with how-to-do-it questions when the play is over. Their visit to the theatre can be made more satisfying if it includes lobby displays of unusual stage properties, costumes, and model stage sets related to the current show or plays they have seen in the past.

Intermediate children have gained sufficient knowledge that they can appreciate the product of careful research. Primary children may enjoy the mystery of "a mythical kingdom in a faraway place," but those at the intermediate level prefer to know that the kingdom was that of King Arthur and the faraway place was England.

Planning for scenic elements that are consistent with the spirit and content of the story calls for some investigation. Knowing your audience will help you determine how to conduct research—whether sources should be storybooks (sometimes children's books are useful resources since the picture illustrations serve a function similar to that of scenery in the children's theatre) or volumes that give more authentic treatment to the realities of history, architecture, and costume.

To serve the production effectively, the design should take on several forms. A floor plan is necessary for the director and actors to work out proper space relationships in rehearsal and will assist the properties people in determining the requirements and limitations established for the elements they will place in the scene. It also becomes a basic guide for those who will mount instruments for lighting and other special effects.

It is impossible to visualize a complete and painted setting from seeing it mapped out on a floor plan. To know the effect toward which all technical crews are working, a perspective drawing or a model—in full color and with all set props shown in place —must be made.

If the play calls for scene changes, the model has great practical value in the working out of the best means of shifting scenery. Complex devices such as revolving stages and scenic units mounted on wagons can be proved workable in miniature before major tasks of construction are undertaken.

If the play calls for scene changes, speed of operation will be a matter of primary concern. Children grow restless if there are delays, and scenery must be designed with that in mind. In planning settings for *The Sleeping Beauty,* the model for which is pictured on the following pages, pieces made carefully to scale established in advance the practicality of speedy scene changes through mounting some pieces on revolving units and flying others into the scene from above. Preparing such a model takes a great deal of time, but most designers find it much easier than attempting such a complex plan on paper.

The designer has one more major assignment, the preparation of working drawings for all new construction; but before that is done, he should check the inventory of flats, levels, step units, etc., to determine what scenic elements are already available. For every show beyond the first one, there almost certainly will be pieces that can be used again.

Working drawings are made to scale and reveal the reverse side of all scenery to be constructed. From them it is possible to determine the amount of lumber, muslin, hardware, etc. that must be purchased and to set up a work schedule for the scenery crew.

That kind of preparation in the children's theatre differs from the basic planning for any good theatre production in only one important way. The children's theatre designers and technicians usually are called upon to exercise more imagination and work with more unusual materials. A wall made of scrim instead of muslin may disappear as light behind it reveals a fairy godmother or a pumpkin coach; a face may appear where moments before there seemed to be an ordinary mirror; a sturdy beanstalk may appear from behind a wall and grow up out of sight. None of those effects is as difficult as it may appear to be, and the challenge to imagination adds an element of fun and excitement. (There may be some comfort in knowing that when imagination fails, books on scenecraft are available that provide virtually all of the answers. Excellent technical aids may be found in several books of this series.[1])

Most special scenic effects require the creative involvement of a lighting crew. The most obvious purpose of stage lighting, of course, is illumination, but the varied play of color and intensity can do much to bring attention where it should be. Action onstage may focus attention, but lighting helps to emphasize the focal point by reducing the intensity in other areas and, through the use of color, to set the mood of the scene.

Shifting attention with light may even be the means of effecting a scene change. Simultaneous staging is a design technique in which two or more settings are placed on the stage at the same time, all in full view of the audience were it not for the use of light to direct attention to the area in which action occurs. It is another device permitting a speedy flow of action from scene to scene without the distraction and delay that might be involved in more complicated scene changes.

Light also may transform the very same setting into something that appears to be quite different if the lighting colors are used

[1] *The Theatre Student • Scenery* by W. Joseph Stell, Richards Rosen Press.

The taunting of a wicked fairy in The Sleeping Beauty . . .

. . . and the benediction of the Fairy Godmother in Cinderella *broke mysteriously into the scene through the use of scrim in the construction of scenery.*

Scrim also gave the Book of Fate its mystic power in The Magic Horn of Charlemagne.

A model of the setting for The Sleeping Beauty *made it possible to see exactly how scenic elements would fit on the stage and how they might best be moved during scene changes.*

Moving two revolving stage units and reversing the door unit, up center, produced the tower scene for The Sleeping Beauty *in a matter of seconds.*

For the forest scene in The Sleeping Beauty, *small revolving units mounted on the larger ones were turned to present a background of forest green. Flat tree units were set in place to complete the scene. (In the actual stage setting these were flown on weight-tested wire and dropped in during the scene change. The center unit contained a scrim panel so that Beauty could sometimes be revealed asleep in the palace during the forest scene.)*

to bring out or to wash out colors that have been used in painting the scene. An area brightly spattered with red and orange, for example, will appear black under the cold light of moonlight blue. Fluorescent paints and fabrics under ultraviolet light will produce even more striking changes.

The most direct way in which light may be used to produce and change scenes is to project scenic elements against a neutral background. Scenic projections may be used in combination with other units of scenery—clouds in the sky or a distant castle, for example—or they may be used to produce the total scene. Although many devices for scene projection can be purchased or rented, probably the easiest to make or borrow are the Linnebach projector (a concentrated filament lamp in a black box) and the kind of overhead projector that is used in classrooms. Either will project whatever is designed on acetate or glass or can be used to project the shadow image of three-dimensional objects placed in front of the light source.

Just as the actors extend action beyond reality when playing for children, and scene designers make imaginative use of color and shape, the lighting technician contributes to theatrical excitement as he produces special effects. As Rumpelstiltskin spins straw into gold, fluorescent materials can be made to glow in the dark through the use of ultraviolet light. Projected images can produce effects that would be difficult to achieve through the use of painted scenery, as when an eerie-looking tree projected into the cemetery scene extends its shadowy arms to frighten Tom Sawyer. Scrim is built into the setting, but it is the light man's hand on the dimmer that reveals the wicked fairy in the tower as she appears in *The Sleeping Beauty*.

Lighting instruments and control equipment can be very expensive items, but for a performing group with limited funds, inexpensive substitutes for theatre spotlights and dimmers are to be had. Simple reflector spotlights and floodlights mounted in swivel sockets will serve, and dimmers can be built at very little cost using crocks filled with a solution of salt or soda as an electrolyte. The response given by an audience of children to the special contribution made by good lighting makes both the effort and the cost worthwhile.

There is something special, too, about

Toy borrowing was a major task for the properties crew in this production of The Puppet Prince.

Scene changes were simplified for The Puppet Prince *by designing similar floor plans for these two settings so that one could be nested against the other.*

Simultaneous staging is a technique for placing more than one setting on stage at once to permit rapid scene change. The scene to the right was the anteroom to the royal bed chamber in The Tinder Box, but it occupied only one half of the stage. Beside it was an exterior scene. Because attention was directed to the desired area with light, the audience never saw two scenes as they appear below.

This image on clear acetate was projected on the cyclorama . . .

. . . to produce the ominous background below for the cemetery scene in Tom Sawyer.

The use of pipe supports with Nu-rail and Rota-lock fittings (See Chapter X and Appendix F) . . .

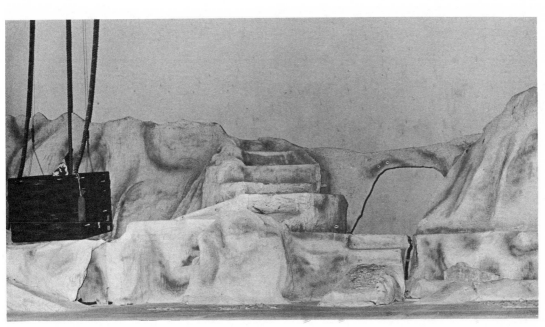

. . . provided sturdy levels and ramps to support vigorous action in The Man in the Moon.

Scenic elements seen in this picture of Pygmalion *in rehearsal* . . .

. . . *may be found in this setting for Piers's Garret in* The Tinder Box—*an example of how time and money can be saved by storing scenic units for future use.*

This water dimmer, designed and built by high-school students, provided flexible lighting control for Barrington High School Children's Theatre productions for several years. Two wires from one side of an electrical circuit placed in a crock of salt or soda solution caused lights to dim as they were drawn apart and brighten as they were moved closer together. (Designed by William Carter)

Plastic foam was used to create a rough-textured surface in the setting for The Man in the Moon.

The properties crew used a fishing reel to draw this four-mouse-power pumpkin coach across the stage in Cinderella.

stage properties and costumes for the children's theatre. A props crew for an adult show never has such an interesting assignment as the making of papier-mâché mice and pumpkin coach, and the costumer for a children's play can hardly be expected to borrow costumes for the three dogs in *The Tinder Box* or the Mock Turtle in *Alice in Wonderland*. Both costumes and properties must be carefully designed, adding variety to the scene but always in harmony with its color and style.

The choice of materials for costumes and upholstery is not limited to the authentic fabrics belonging to a place or period. There may well be visually effective substitutes that will better serve both the budget and the needs of a young audience. Children like shiny, colorful materials, and their use can aid the director in developing spectacular scenes as well as in focusing attention on a center of interest.

Fabric houses supply a great variety of materials to meet special needs. "Bunny fur" for animal costumes, jewel cloth for sparkling costume decoration, velveteen or chiffon velvet for royal robes, and even fluorescent materials that glow in the dark under

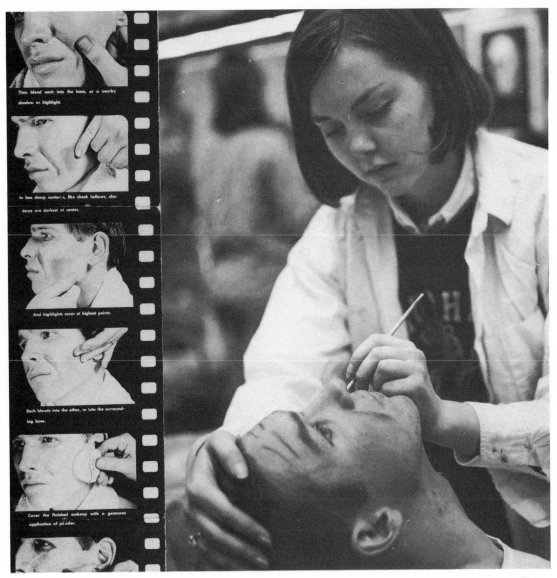

The student shown here observed the application of highlights and shadows in Paramount's film-strip on makeup (See Appendix F) and then practiced what she had learned.

ultraviolet light are available in a variety of colors and patterns. To save money, one may buy the makings for jewel cloth, dye inexpensive fabrics in brilliant colors, spatter any material with scene paint to give the illusion of texture, and even produce fluorescence by laundering a costume in a detergent before it is displayed on stage under ultraviolet light.

If storage space is available, a continuing children's theatre program can make repeated use of many costumes and properties by making simple alterations. Like the scene designer, in the interest of saving both time and money, costumes and properties people should check the inventory before purchasing materials and assigning tasks.

Makeup for the children's theatre often goes beyond the basic techniques of theatrical makeup. The principles of highlight and shadow used on any stage apply, of course, but animals and the fanciful characters often found in children's plays call for the use of unusual materials and a lively imagination.

Using cotton and latex, an actor's face

Following a makeup technique developed by Irene Corey (See Bibliography) troggles in The Man in the Moon *were made to appear the "rabbity things" called for by the playwright.*

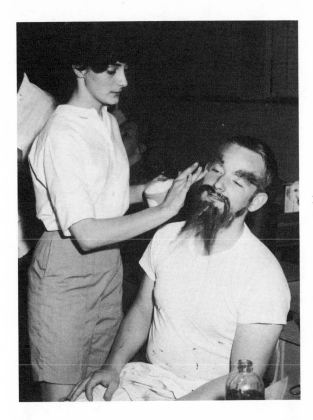

The careful application of crepe hair in make-up . . .

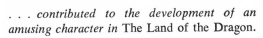

. . . contributed to the development of an amusing character in The Land of the Dragon.

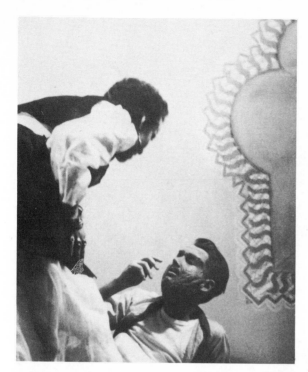

A flexible half mask was constructed of cotton and latex to make Cassim appear fatter than he was in Ali Baba and the Forty Thieves.

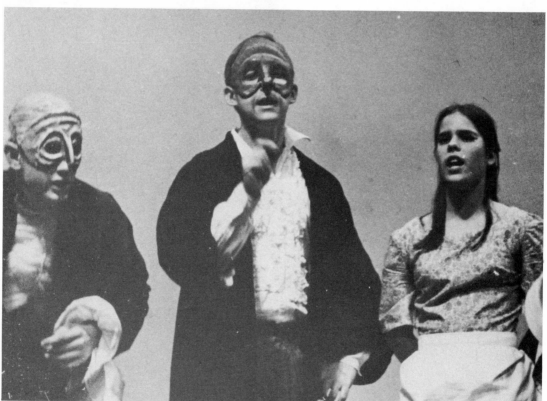

Inflexible half masks of Celastic were used in The Magic Isle *for characters cast in the tradition of Commedia dell'Arte.*

A sound crew playing appropriate recorded music and sound effects can contribute much to the mood and excitement of a play for children. All cues must be marked, and the script must be followed carefully during performance.

Cotton and latex constructions added length to the chin and nose of the Grand Duchess in Greensleeves' Magic.

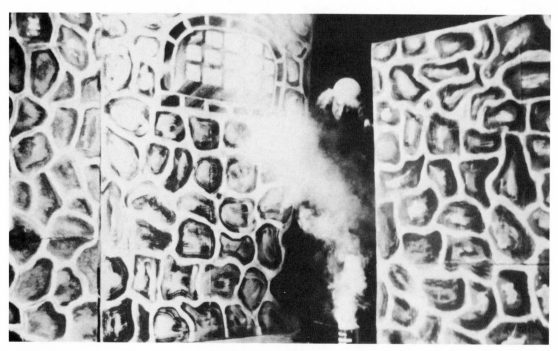

The disappearance of a character in a flash of light and a puff of smoke is often called for in the children's theatre. Care must be taken in placing powder in a flash pot so as not to create a danger to the actor involved. A very small quantity will produce a good effect.

can be changed to assume almost any shape while still retaining enough flexibility to permit normal mouth movement. Other materials such as nose putty, plastic wax, crepe hair, and pieces cut from rubber masks also find frequent use. Regular stage makeup usually provides color for facial features and other exposed parts of the body, whereas sometimes such materials as bunny fur or other fabrics are applied with liquid latex. To make bear features for Pooh in *Winnie-the-Pooh,* for example, a face shape might be built of cotton and latex, covered with brown bunny fur, and topped with a Ping-Pong-ball nose.

Most professional actors do their own makeup, and performers in the amateur children's theatre may do so. Usually, however, a crew is organized, and they work to develop the special skills necessary if imaginative makeup is to have an important influence on the child audience.

The final two weeks of the rehearsal schedule should be spent in vitalizing the spirit of teamwork as cast and crews coordinate their efforts. Scene changes must be carefully timed, and light and sound cues rehearsed until all are a part of a common involvement in the action of the play. The goal is a dress rehearsal that can run as smoothly as the final performance.

When actors first appear in costume and makeup on a completed stage set under effective lighting and can respond believably to the offstage sounds and other special effects, a profound feeling of mutual admiration develops. Actors perform better because so many things contribute to *belief,* and the sense of purpose that had existed only as motivation for specialized efforts has new meaning for each crew member as actors breathe life into the products of their creative involvement.

In the final dress rehearsal, all feel the rich promise of laughter, excitement, and applause that will come when the audience joins the team and the theatre experience is complete.

Chapter VIII

CREATIVE PLAY-MAKING

Although most play productions invite creative effort only in the developing of characters, the manner of directing them in the unfolding events of the play, and in the many technical details that contribute to its effectiveness, a further possibility is that of having the play itself created by those who will bring it to the stage.

The most obvious way for a theatre to produce an original play is to have a resident playwright. He may be the director, a member of the company, or a writer who joins the team in order to see his work performed. Another approach, however, is to depart from the tradition of a script and, through improvisation, to evolve your own unique treatment of a familiar story, an unusual event, or an original idea.

The source of an idea may be in a poem, an experience, or an observable truth. The idea may include or imply the manner of its telling, or it may struggle a long time in groping for appropriate dramatic form. It may occur as a flash of insight in the mind of one person, or it may grow out of a probing exchange of thoughts and feelings —perhaps even out of the heat of argument. Whatever the manner of its development, it should emerge as an idea worth sharing and capable of generating enthusiasm in those who will turn it into a theatre experience.

In creating a play through improvisation, a group of people is involved in the dynamics of directing diverse sensory, emotional, intellectual, and physical energies toward the attaining of common insights and the reaching of a common goal. The director in such a group cannot plan ahead for the specifics of scene development. Rather, he serves as an adviser, questioner, and evaluator—a kind of catalyst to the process. As midwife in the birth of a new play, he can contribute aid and comfort to ease its arrival, but he cannot predict with any accuracy what it will be. In fact, the exciting spontaneity of a creative act may be crippled by the imposing of authoritarian control.

The process begins with group discussion. Perhaps with one person as the initiator of an idea, the group seeks to define some *fundamental truth* or *impression of human experience* that can be demonstrated theatrically and then tries to determine the nature of *events* that will reveal the impression or truth, what kinds of *characters* will be needed to make them believable, and what kind of *conflict* will develop. Then events are allowed to unfold through *improvisation* and discussion, and the actors "discover" the play together.

Some exercises in improvisation serve well as background for creative play-making and, indeed, as training for the actor in any kind of performance. As aids, you may wish to consult such sources as Viola Spolin's *Improvisation for the Theatre, Acting Is Believing* by Charles McGaw, and *A Course Guide in Theatre Arts at the Secondary School Level* published by the American Educational Theatre Association.

Briefly, the exercises involve actors' responding imaginatively to a set of given circumstances. Given a time, a place, a role, a prescribed activity, and appropriate motivations or goals, they *behave* in a manner consistent with the circumstances. Their actions and dialogue should be natural and free of any concern for audience response. Any attempt to give an "impressive" performance detracts from *belief,* which is the primary goal.

One way to reduce the tendency to "put on an act" is to begin by involving a group in simultaneous response to sideline coaching. If all are milling about freely and there is no "stage" on which to focus audience attention, each actor can become completely responsive to his own imagination. Thus he may effect changes in his environment; create traits of personality, character, attitude, age, and health; and react to imagined stimuli with a variety of emotional responses. With such activity as a recent memory, he may make the transition to improvisation onstage with greater belief in the imaginary stimuli to which he must respond.

Exercises in improvisation may, in fact, provide some ideas for original plays. Impressed by the memory of some conflict that developed or some insight that was gained during an improvised scene, a group may see it as the inciting incident or, perhaps, the climax of a play that could emerge out of improvising a series of related events.

Important to the development of such a play is recognition that the evolutionary growth of a *script* is not the goal. It is the creation of a purposeful theatre experience. The sharing of the experience with an audience occurs when the play is *ready to be written.*

In fact, if there is to be a script at all, it may well be the *product of the performance.* One approach is to tape-record the show and take the recording back to the cast for evaluative discussion and improvised demonstration of suggested refinements and improvements. Then, with performance and evaluation as background, a "playwright" may bring the play to the typewriter and seek to put it in a form that may be meaningful to other groups wishing to use it as the basis for more conventional production.

In the Georgia Governor's Honors Program, as many as fourteen such original plays have been produced within an eight-week summer session. Some lived their brief life on the stage, providing a learning experience for the performing group and pleasure to a single audience. Others have gone through the final stage of development and have become manuscripts, which can now be used in conventional play productions.

Plays in the Georgia program were performed for a teen-age audience. The same technique has been employed with equal success, however, for children. At the Eastside Theatre in St. Paul, Minnesota, many shows have been created from loosely constructed scenarios by a process of improvisation in rehearsal leading to the development of a performance script. Craig Sherfenberg, managing director of the theatre, sees an advantage for the actor in this approach as he extends his creative involvement in the making of a play and is freed from the struggle to learn lines that are "verbally uncomfortable" for him.

In seeking ideas for improvised plays, you may want to borrow thoughts from authors who have succeeded in reaching a child audience through narrative fiction or even biography or history. In exploring that kind of source, however, you may find that much is lost if you borrow an idea without also borrowing the style.

A theatrical technique for staging narrative literature without losing the narrative flavor and the unique qualities that have made an author appealing has been developed by Robert Breen of Northwestern University. It is called Chamber Theatre.

In Chamber Theatre the story remains a narrative and continues to be told in the first or third person just as the author intended. It differs from the recitation or oral reading of the story in that the characters appear as in a play and, if the author has included some events that develop through direct discourse with no interrupting narrative, they may speak dialogue in the same

To provide theatre by and for youth, improvisation is a valuable technique. Students in the Georgia Governor's Honors Program are shown here in their own original version of Antigone, *improvised in a style which made an ancient legend relevant to a twentieth-century experience.*

manner as actors in a play. But it is not a play in the usual sense because characters go beyond dialogue and speak about their thoughts and feelings if the narrative calls for them to do so, and some details may be told by a storyteller who represents the author in third-person narration.

Another departure from conventional dramatic style is the Chamber Theatre use of indirect discourse. Here the action and emotional tone of dialogue are maintained as the actor remains a character interacting with other characters—but in the language of the story as the author has presented it. Some actors may, at first, feel uncomfortable with the style, complaining that "People don't talk that way." *But storytellers do.* When they realize that Chamber Theatre is a form of storytelling, they can adjust comfortably to its unique performance style.

Even third-person narration may sometimes be handled by a character in Chamber Theatre production. If the story is being told by an omniscient observer who reports not only the descriptive detail of events but the inner feelings and motivations of char-

acters, the characters themselves may pick up that part of the narration that reports on themselves. You may well imagine how much of insight, excitement, and authentic emotional power can be given to language that reveals something about a character when it is heard in the character's own voice. The actor at such a moment in the story must regard himself as a storyteller who *talks about* the character while *being* the character.

Except for those times when a character reports self-revealing narration, the third-person narrative requires the presence of a storyteller who is responsive to the developing mood and action but does not interact with other characters. In effect, he plays the author, seeing the action from his point of view and regarding the characters with his degree of insight.

One of the advantages of Chamber Theatre is that it makes available to a performing group the work of some of the finest writers for children. Only a small fraction of deserving children's stories have been rewritten as plays, and they necessarily have sacrificed some of the descriptive detail and transitional narrative that endeared the original works to their readers. The technique makes it possible to bring such authors as Lewis Carroll and Robert Louis Stevenson to the stage in their original forms and with an added vitality made possible through theatre performance.[1]

Experimentation in the development of new forms and new theatrical styles may borrow freely from the ideas and experiments of others as long as copyrights are not violated. In pursuing any of those innovative forms, however, permission must be obtained if an author is to be quoted directly.

An approach to storytelling that does not draw upon language of the original is the development of improvised scenes linked together by original narrative material. That was done in a Barrington High School production of *The Wizard of Oz* after a play-selection committee had difficulty in deciding which of several published dramatizations they wished to present. They liked some of the ideas in each play studied, but, with no clear preference, they decided to develop their own.

To retain the narrative flavor, an introduction and transitional details between scenes were written in verse form to be presented by a storyteller—performing like the narrator in Chamber Theatre. Then, with continuing reference to the L. Frank Baum original, the cast improvised action and dialogue that would present theatrically the main thrust of the story's complication.

The following scenario linked by the storyteller's verses describes the product that resulted:

Storyteller.
'Twas many and many a year ago.

[1] An example of Chamber Theatre adaption for the children's theatre is Lois Lenski's story, *Indian Captive: The Story of Mary Jemison*, adapted by Gertrude Breen and published by the Coach House Press, Chicago.

The thunder roared and the wind did
  blow.
In cities and towns, on farms and on
  ranches.
It blew down the trees and blew off
  the branches.
All the chickens were cold; it had
  blown off their feathers!
You never have seen such terrible
  weather!
But feathers weren't needed; even
  horses could fly!
Just taking a casual look at the sky,
You never knew what you might see
  sailing by.
The big wind gave all things a brand
  new location,
And that's why we see here this strange
  combination:
A scarecrow and fence 'round a corn-
  field that grew there
With a girl, dog, and house that appear
  to be new there.
The poor girl's not pleased with a big
  storm that lands us
On a Munchkinland farm that is far,
  far from Kansas.

Dorothy and Toto meet the Munchkins and discover that their house has landed on the Wicked Witch of the East. They meet the Witch of the North who provides background information and tells of the great Wizard who lives in the Emerald City. She gives Dorothy the silver shoes that had been worn by the Wicked Witch of the East. As Dorothy is about to leave, the Scarecrow begins to move and speak, telling of his need for brains. Dorothy, Toto, and the Scarecrow set out down the Yellow Brick Road to find Oz and seek his help in getting back to Kansas and in securing a brain for the Scarecrow.

As they travel, they meet a Tin Woodman and, after oiling his jaws so he can speak, learn of his need for a heart. Then they are attacked by a Lion, and Dorothy

The Storyteller's involvement in the action she described contributed to the excitement of an original Wizard of Oz *adaptation.*

proves him a coward. With courage for the Cowardly Lion as an added objective, all set out together to seek the Wizard of Oz.

Storyteller.
What a wonderful group of good friends Dorothy found
When that terrible storm put her down on the ground.
(When people are good, they have good friends around them.
I think that is really the reason she found them.)
And no one has ever had better intention
Than Dorothy and Toto—and these friends that I mention.
They'll ask the great Wizard to change what they seem to be
Into exactly what each one has dreamed to be.

They meet an old farmer who gives directions and further information about the Wizard's mysterious powers.

They arrive at the palace and are stopped by the Guardian of the Gates. He provides green glasses, which must be worn by everyone who enters the Emerald City, and directs them to Oz, the Great and Terrible.

Oz appears (behind scrim) as a great head and offers help only on the condition that they destroy the Wicked Witch of the West.

Storyteller.
The wicked old Witch had no wish for the guests
Who followed the sun to her home in the West.
In the land of the Winkies, she hatched a dark plot
To see that those seeking to find her would not.

The Wicked Witch of the West (appearing in a spot of light) calls upon her wolves to attack.

Storyteller.
They sought first the Tin Woodman and finally found him
With all of his friends standing frightened around him.
But the Woodman stood bravely to meet the attack.
He raised up his axe, and he beat the wolves back.

The Witch calls her crows to attack.

Storyteller.
But our friend, Mr. Scarecrow, as good as his name,
Was as brave as the Woodman and gave them the same.
Forty great crows flew in for a peck,
And as each one flew by him, he twisted its neck.

The Witch calls her bees to sting them.

Storyteller.
The Scarecrow, you know, had plenty of straw.
It seems strange that, having no brain, still he saw
In an instant what had to be done.
With nowhere to hide and no time to run,
He told Dorothy and Lion to lie there beside him,
And he'd cover them up with the straw stuffed inside him.
That left the Tin Woodman to stay and be stung,
But he left those bees lying helpless among
The leaves and the straw that the Scarecrow had scattered.
Their stingers were bent and their stingers were battered.
(If a bee tried to sting you or me, he'd get in,
But the sting of a bee cannot penetrate tin.)

The Witch arms her slaves with spears and sends them off to attack.

Storyteller.
> She sent out the Winkies; each one was her slave,
> But the weak little Winkies were not half as brave
> As the Cowardly Lion, who let out a ROAR
> That sent them all running, afraid there'd be more.
> They returned to the Witch and reported the meeting.

Witch.
> Go and get me a strap, and I'll give you a beating.

Dorothy encounters the Witch in her castle.

When the Witch tries to steal her silver shoes, Dorothy throws water, the one thing that will destroy her.

Storyteller.
> Just a word now to help you keep up with the plot:
> The Witch was destroyed, but her magic was not.
> Magic powers were held in a cap made of gold.
> With the Wicked Witch gone, it was Dorothy's to hold.
> She used it to wish for some monkeys with wings.
> (And a magical cap can do marvelous things.)
> They appeared in an instant, flew them off with a swish

When Dorothy and Toto prepared to leave Munchkinland and go down the Yellow Brick Road, they met the first of their traveling companions propped up on a pole. Dialogue developed easily, based on the scenario that outlined this event in the story.

To the Wizard who'd promised to grant
    each a wish.

Back at the palace of the Emerald City, they report their success to Oz and ask him to keep his promises. He reveals the fact that he has no great power to grant their wishes, but they insist that promises must be kept. Stalling for time, he asks them to return the next day.

Storyteller.
    When a promise is made, it should al-
        ways be kept.
    That thought gave the Wizard bad
        dreams as he slept.
    He was a good man, but he had no
        great power;
    And that worried his mind as he came
        to the hour
    When promises made must be followed
        by deeds
    That will answer each visitor's personal
        needs.
    Although three asked for qualities
        growing inside,
    The kind of thing each in himself could
        provide,
    Sweet Dorothy seemed headed for news
        that was tragic
    Unless he could locate some powerful
        magic.
    Putting off till tomorrow what has to
        be done
    Makes one worry longer and spoils all
        his fun.
    After one night of worry—just to have
        a delay,
    What he promised "tomorrow" must
        be given TODAY!

Oz goes through the ritual of presenting symbolic brain, heart, and courage to the Scarecrow, Woodman, and Lion. Then they help him break the news to Dorothy that he still cannot keep his promise.

Advised by the Guardian of the Gates to seek help from Glinda, the good witch of the South, they set out for the land of the Quadlings where she lives.

Storyteller.
    With friends who were loyal and friends
        who were true,
    Dorothy knew she had nothing to fear;
        she'd get through.
    They packed up to leave on the very
        next day,
    Said goodbye to the Wizard and were
        off and away
    To the land of the Quadlings and
        Glinda the Good—
    The one person left in this strange land
        who could
    Get her out of the place where the
        cyclone had blown
    And send her back home to the loved
        ones she'd known.
    She faced dangers aplenty, but with
        good friends around,
    She came through the forest and finally
        found
    The land of the Quadlings and Glinda
        the Kind—
    The good witch whose wisdom would
        help her to find
    The place that had never been far from
        her mind.

Glinda tells Dorothy that the magic shoes that she took from the Wicked Witch of the East and is now wearing have the power to take her anywhere—and she could have gone home on the very day she first arrived in Munchkinland.

After fond farewells, Dorothy uses the power of her shoes to leave her friends and return to Kansas, where she is reunited with a worried Aunt Em and Uncle Henry.

Much of the dialogue was directly inspired by the language of the original story, but active imaginations responding in character produced humor as well as inventive conversation and action that were unique to the stage adaptation. Although some ideas had to be ruled out as being inconsistent, repetitive, or theatrically ineffective, it occurred infrequently once the characters became believable. When actors are thinking and listening in character, they are not likely to behave or speak in an inappropriate manner.

Another unique approach to original play-making was used in telling the story of *Alice in Wonderland*. Intended for a junior-high-school audience, it even had a change of title and was called *Alice in Retrospect*.

The unusual feature of the production was its double cast—one to be seen and one to be heard. For each role but Alice, one person was cast because his voice was right for an animated interpretation of the role, and the other was cast because in appearance and in pantomime ability he was visually effective. The "voices" could be seen sitting before microphones on side stages where they were able to observe the action. Their counterparts onstage synchronized lip movement to the spoken dialogue but were primarily concerned with being physically involved. Technical crews were

There always is room for original ideas in the children's theatre. In Alice in Retrospect *the Cheshire Cat was not an actor at all but an off-stage voice and this plywood cutout flying in from above.*

equally concerned with being visually effective, and the result was a lively audience involvement in an unusual theatre experience.

Creating a play by drawing upon the imaginations of a group requires a spirit of freedom to experiment and a willingness to invite changes from day to day. Although that may seem quite different from conventional work with published plays, it has some things in common with the experience of working with a resident playwright.

Rarely is the finished manuscript for a good play the product of quiet reverie. Certainly a playwright spends long hours in thought and in conversation with his typewriter, but the first draft of a play is seldom the last. It is an untried idea, waiting to be tested.

To meet the test, it must leave the quiet of the playwright's study and go out to meet people. It enters the world as a brainchild, adored by its parent, but it soon becomes a social being that must make adjustments if it hopes to get along with a company of actors and a director who seeks to bring play and players into a common experience.

The playwright probably expects to find that what he created as a thing of beauty has faults and weaknesses. When they are revealed by the efforts of an acting company, he returns to his typewriter to add, delete, and repair. The result is a play better adjusted to the talents of players who will perform it.

The process may, in fact, be repeated many times over as rehearsals cast their revealing light on the growing brainchild taking its first steps. Performers working with a resident playwright learn to expect the unexpected as their scripts grow heavy with revised scenes, and their minds grow weary with the confusion of new dialogue to learn. Sometimes, if the playwright is a good listener, the actors contribute to the changes as emerging characters begin "doing what comes naturally."

The real test of the play comes when its social circle widens to include an audience. Then the playwright really has a chance to observe how well his child is getting along. Again he may find that some adjustments are needed. Perhaps the audience becomes restless during a talky scene or something is misunderstood or an unexpected laugh reveals that the audience has picked up an unintended meaning. So he seeks a way to break up lengthy speeches or adds a transitional scene to improve understanding or deletes an offending word that held a double meaning for the audience.

Ultimately the play passes its audience test as changes are incorporated into later performances. The product at the end of the play's run has made its adjustment to both the cast and the audience and is ready to be reproduced for use with other casts and other audiences—perhaps even to be submitted to a publisher.

But suppose the play had taken its first steps in rehearsal with a different company of actors under a different director. Or suppose the play had met a different audience, more or less sophisticated than the one that inspired those final adjustments. Under either condition, it seems likely that the changes made by the playwright would have been different. Perhaps some would not have been made at all.

Thus it seems likely that whatever published play you select was written for actors —but not your actors. They played for an audience of children, but they may have been different in many ways from the children for whom you will perform. It may sometimes be desirable, therefore, to make some purposeful adjustments of your own.

Clearly, no alterations should be made that in any way obscure or deny the essential truths revealed in the play or distort the playwright's intention. It still is his baby, and he has an understandable interest in protecting it from those who would make it their own. To ensure the suitability of your

production, any major changes should be made only with permission of the copyright owner.

There are some valid reasons for making adjustments, often related to the special talents, limitations, or purpose of your organization. The play may call for dance numbers, and you have no dancers. There may be some special musical talent in your group that you think could be used to good advantage. You may not have enough people to provide the "extras" called for or the right proportion of boys and girls to cast the play without changing the beggar to a beggarwoman. Knowing your audience, you may realize that the language used in a scene will produce a laugh where the playwright did not intend humor. Recognizing the value of the play in providing training and experience for your actors, you may want to add "extras" or add to their importance by giving them more to say and do. Time limitations may force some cuts, which, in turn, require the addition of an original narrative bridge between scenes.

Ideally, of course, you choose a play that suits your players and your audience so that rehearsals may proceed smoothly and remain faithful to the playwright's published script. That, indeed, is what happens most of the time. The following, however, are examples of purposeful changes that helped players to make effective use of their talents in achieving the playwright's intention.

To balance the strong feelings of danger generated by the sinister scheming in *Ali Baba and the Forty Thieves,* we introduced a comic element by giving the two gong bearers a simple comic sequence to play. The play had a built-in narrator so the gong bearers could concern themselves exclusively with the business of striking the gongs.

Cast in the roles were two girls, one tiny and one very tall. The little girl was the inept apprentice who, in a series of appearances before five scenes, developed competence. As the house lights dimmed, both girls came on stage and played the following brief scene:

Gong Bearer. (Rings gong. Then looks sternly at the Apprentice.)

Apprentice. Bong.

Gong Bearer. (To audience) This is an Oriental play, and as it starts, two Oriental gongs should ring. But my small assistant seems to think it is her job to sing.

Apprentice. Excuse me, but I'd much prefer to watch the play instead.

Gong Bearer. You beat upon the gong, my girl, or I'll beat upon your head.

Apprentice. (Runs off R. Returns with gong, strikes it, and runs off.)

Gong Bearer. (Exits L. with stately step as the curtains part.)

Before the second scene, they appeared again, and as the Gong Bearer stood formally by, her apprentice spoke to the audience:

Apprentice. To ring a gong should take some practice,
But, pardon me, the simple fact is
I'm just learning how to play,
So please be kind to me today.

Gong Bearer. Play!
(Both strike gongs and march off R. and L.)

To open scene three, the Gong Bearer entered alone. Then the Apprentice entered late and, properly frightened of the consequences, struck a proper pose, and both struck their gongs and marched off.

Evidence of progress in the Apprentice's training could be seen before the next scene as both entered formally and on time. The Gong Bearer raised her stick above the gong, then waited for the Apprentice who still was tardy on this important cue.

For the final scene, the Apprentice performed without a flaw. Enthusiastic applause from the young audience indicated how much they had identified with her in the development of this simple incidental plot.

Transitional devices in the form of act openers are found frequently in children's theatres. Some companies use a stock character, perhaps an animal or a clown, who appears with every children's play to offer whatever commentary or narrative may seem desirable in directing attention toward the stage and in bringing the play and audience closer together. In other groups, the director becomes a familiar figure as he appears before each play in the role of host.

If a group is not tied to such a tradition, the play itself can dictate the approach, and the playwright's ideas become a stimulus to imagination and the basis for whatever original devices may seem desirable—as in the case of the gong bearers cited above.

Perhaps a more important adjustment in *Ali Baba and the Forty Thieves* was made within the play itself. It was written in 1947 by very competent playwrights. If they were writing it at the present time, it seems reasonable to suppose that their work might reflect recent thinking about the desirability of a more moderate approach to violence. Two scenes in the play involve a kind of horror that could be suggested less vividly through the exercise of imagination.

The first occurs when the robber chieftain, Hassan, has Cassim, the greedy brother of Ali Baba, trapped in his cave. In threatening tones he says:

He hides within, the scurvy knave, but he shall die within, for with my knife I'll quarter him, like this, and this! (He demonstrates slashing his own body into quarters. The robbers growl and brandish their knives. Hassan motions them to remain, then with knife uplifted he steps into the cave. Everything is quiet. Then we hear Cassim's agonized scream, a thud, and in a moment Hassan steps out. His knife is red. He wipes the knife on his scarf, sheaths it in his belt, then mo-

tions the robbers to put back the gold.
They do so. Hassan steps before the rock.)

O cave, you hold a bloody blob,
Of one who sought to steal and rob,
Woe unto him who learns our magic,
To him will come an end most tragic.

The impact of this bloody image was lessened by turning to magic rather than violent action. Taking some license with the original story, we extended the power of the word *Sesame* and used it to dispatch Cassim without bloodshed. The following verse replaced the one quoted above and made the frightening business and sounds unnecessary:

Nay, better still—and more absurd,
I'll quarter him with magic words. (Robbers laugh.)
O, Sesame, cut his bones in twain;
   (A puff of smoke comes from the cave.)
Now slice across him once again.
   (Another puff of smoke is seen.)
By magic, one is turned to four
And wrapped like sausage in a store.
   (Laughter.)

With only minor adjustments (saying Cassim was "divided" instead of "slashed," for example), the dialogue then proceeded as written, and children were not left with the image of a cruel and bloody murder.

Without completely eliminating the familiar story of bandits hidden in oil jars and the trick that destroyed them, the impact of suffering and death was removed by turning once again to verse and magic, which accomplished the victory over the bandits who waited in hiding. Again simple changes in dialogue eliminated specific reference to the violent action, and where the stage direction called for pouring in the boiling oil, Morgiana spoke the magic verse, calling upon the power of Sesame:

O, Sesame, make these bandits boil,
And let each jar be filled with oil.

Instead of the suffering groans and howls indicated in the script, the magic was evidenced by a flash and a puff of smoke from each jar.

Shortly after the episode with the oil jars, Morgiana was expected once again to murder when, as a part of her dance, she was directed to plunge a dagger into the breast of Hassan, the bandit chief. To avoid that kind of violent display, she again turned in verse to the magic powers of Sesame:

To entertain and play a joke,
I'll bind you up with magic rope.
   (She dances in circles around Hassan, as though to bind him with invisible rope.)
O, Sesame, make this magic real
And bind him tight enough to feel!

Several advantages were gained by the changes made in the script of *Ali Baba and the Forty Thieves*. First, the art of theatre always is well served when suggestion can take the place of obvious disclosure. It gives the audience an opportunity to imagine rather than simply to absorb. Second, children were saved a disquieting experience with present violence. Thus was produced not only a more orderly involvement in a theatre experience but more desirable afterthoughts and behaviors beyond the moment of the play. Third, Morgiana, a sweet and gentle girl, was relieved of action quite inconsistent with her character. Her rescue of Ali Baba was courageous, but not vicious or cruel.

Special talents in a producing organization sometimes can point the direction that adjustments in a published manuscript will take. If a group has an especially capable dancer, perhaps a dance number can be added or expanded; a special effect may be based on someone's special skill as a magician; musical talent may permit the enriching of the theatre experience with song.

When doing *The Tinder Box,* we were fortunate to have a student who was interested in composing music. That led us to solving the problem of finding a suitable ending for the play.

Alan Broadhurst wrote the play for children in Yorkshire, England, and directed it himself. No doubt, he knew the audience and wrote effectively for them, for the play was an outstanding success. Yet, knowing our audience, we questioned the effectiveness of ending with a "Hip, hip—Hooray!" for each character. We wanted to retain the proud and joyous spirit of cheering but to direct it more specifically into thoughts of the total play. Our solution was original music and a song that wove threads of the plot together.

After the swordplay, we used the first of the cheers provided and continued to the following original conclusion:

Voice 1. Hooray for Johannes. Hip, hip—
All. Hooray!
Voice 2. What do you think of your common soldier now, your majesty?
Voice 3. And what do *you* think of him, Princess? (General laughter.)
Princess. (Singing) I've heard that a soldier's a man who is bad,
    That if I should meet one, the king would be sad,
    That my heart would break and my mother would cry—
    But I don't believe a word—no, no, not I!
King. I've heard that a king is a man who is wise
    With a brain that would fit a crown— just this size,
    (Removes crown.)
    Whose bravery's a legend that never could die,
    But now I'm not quite so sure—no, no, not I.
Johannes. I've heard that true love will make each man a king,
    (King places crown on Johannes.)

And love is the theme of the song that I sing.
    I'll stand by your side as the long years go by.
    I'll never stop loving you—no, no, not I!
All. With courage and truth, he's brought joy to our land.
    Against him the forces of evil can't stand.
    We'll rally around him and shout to the sky!
Bosun. Will any oppose him?
All. No, no! Not I!

Several approaches have been suggested here for reaching your children's theatre audience. Having determined the unique characteristics and needs of your theatre, you will in most instances find a published play that meets your requirements. Sometimes, however, you will find a play that seems admirably suited to your needs if, with a little applied imagination, you make minor purposeful adjustments. And, sooner or later, your imagination probably will cut free of any published play to produce a theatre experience that is the unique product of your group.

This is not intended to be an exhaustive treatment of ways to put the stamp of originality on the products of your theatre. Originality, by its very nature, is without limit. Nor have we intended to suggest that most plays need adjustments or that directors are free to tamper irresponsibly with the playwright's property. Any kind of major change requires correspondence with the publisher and permission of the copyright owner.

Theatre, however, is a creative art. Playwrights create plays; actors create characters; directors create believable events. Together they create a theatre experience for an audience. It is a dynamic process, and within it are many variables—adjustable to the unique demands of your theatre.

Chapter IX

THE MAGIC MOMENT

All that has gone before is preparation for the time when the play and audience meet. There is more to that meeting, however, than a magic moment in the theatre. Contact with your audience really occurs in three phases—before, during, and after the performance. Or perhaps the three experiences might better be called *anticipation, realization,* and *reflection.*

Anticipating an audience involves more than thoughts of excited youngsters descending the steps of school buses and their laughter and applause during their hour in the theatre. There is pleasure in such thinking, but there is greater purpose and pleasure, too, in more direct preperformance contact with the audience.

The excitement of anticipation should be shared by the prospective audience and will be if you make meaningful contact with the children you serve prior to the date of the show. A part of it is, of course, the usual distribution of posters to schools and store windows and publication of pictures and stories in the local papers. By its nature, however, the children's theatre invites a more creative approach to preparing the audience for the performance.

Because an active imagination is one of the major assets teen-agers bring to the theatre, there is good reason to expect that the details of publicity and business management in a youth theatre will go beyond the usual and customary arrangements. It is important to recognize the value to be gained by placing those responsibilities in the hands of young people rather than just assigning committees to do the bidding of

the director. Their enthusiasm is an important ingredient in working out the details of reaching the audience with information and tickets and even with bringing the play itself to them on tour and with guiding them to their seats when they come to the theatre.

Theatre experience plays a significant part in the education of children. Teachers and parents, therefore, also share in the excitement of anticipating a children's theatre production. With some applied imagination, publicity people will find ways to involve them directly in preparing the child audience for a more meaningful visit to the theatre.

Teaching aids offering historical information, suggested references, and materials to be handled or used by students are always welcome and can be useful in stimulating curiosity or improving understanding. One good way to introduce characters and establish something of their relationships to one another is to prepare coloring books showing sketches of some of the principal characters and captions or verses that help to stimulate interest in them.

If the play involves the use of strange materials or strange words that can be made clear by demonstration, sending physical properties into the classrooms for examination or use can be helpful. Before a production of *Little Lee Bobo,* for example, the cast visited Chicago's Chinatown and purchased joss sticks and red paper notices. We retained enough for use in rehearsals and performances and sent the rest into classrooms where the joss sticks could be burned and the notices examined. Teachers

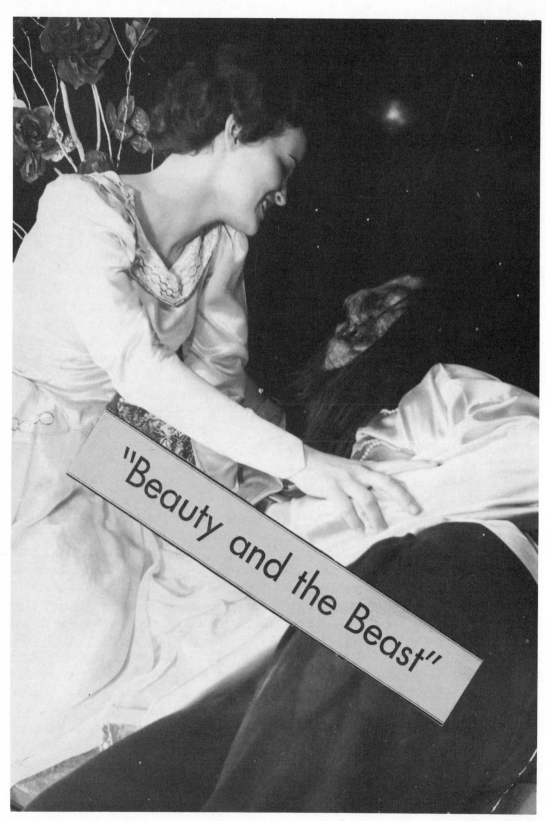

One of the most appealing devices for advertising a play is to offer a sneak preview of things to come through the display of a photograph.

GREENSLEEVES IS A LIVELY
FELLOW—
THE SPIRIT OF
SONG, LAUGHTER,
AND DANCE

a

HE GOES TO A LAND
WHERE EVERYONE IS
VERY SAD

b

THEY ARE SAD BECAUSE . . .
. . . FITZSNEEZE
AND
THE
GRAND
DUCHESS,
TWO VERY EVIL PEOPLE,
HAVE STOLEN
LAUGHTER, SONG,
AND DANCE
FROM THE KINGDOM!!

c

"GREENSLEEVES' MAGIC"
Tells what happens when
"goodness" meets "evil"
face to face

f

THE KING AND QUEEN
ARE SAD!

d

THE PRINCESSES ARE SAD

e

Children gain some preliminary involvement in the play if a coloring book helps them to antici-
pate its coming.

found that the handling of the items and smelling the joss sticks as they were burned excited an interest in Chinese customs and opened the way to worthwhile class discussions and activity in addition to heightening interest in the play. Later, when joss sticks and red paper notices appeared as props in the performance, the audience had the added excitement of relating them to their own recent experience.

Another stimulating preperformance event is classroom visits by members of the cast in costume a few days before the performance. Children delight in the opportunity to meet and talk with them and are drawn intimately into the play by the sight of familiar figures.

Such a visit is more effective if it is allowed to develop informally, and visiting groups should be small enough so that each performer can figure prominently in the appearance. To ensure consistency of purpose, each visitor should be given a set of instructions such as the following:

1. Stop first at the school office to learn which classes are expecting you. Visit only those rooms for which permission has been given.
2. In the classroom your purpose is to stimulate interest in the play and an understanding of the character you play, not to offer a preview of scenes or to tell the playwright's story. Improvise dialogue that centers on the theme and locale of the play, expressing only those thoughts and attitudes that are characteristic of your role. Involve children in the dialogue if possible by asking relevant questions or addressing them directly. Even during the discussion, stay in character.
3. Don't overstay your welcome. A few minutes will accomplish your purpose. Before leaving, express pleasure in the visit and in the anticipated performance where you will meet again. Be

sure they know when and where the play will be given.

As a part of your visit or independent of it, you may be able to arrange for a display in each school's learning center or library. Children become excited by an opportunity to examine a model set or an exhibit of unusual stage properties or costumes.

Sometimes a reverse of the classroom visit idea is possible, and children come to the theatre for a preview of the stage setting and a look behind the scenes. The visitors may be a class, a Scout troop, or some other organization that anticipates group attendance at the play. One word of caution, however: No unsupervised groups of children should be allowed onstage. In satisfying their curiosity, they might become a demolition squad, and the play would be sadly crippled or indefinitely postponed.

Although schools are the most likely places to meet the future audience, do not overlook the possibility of visiting civic and religious groups working with children. In any case, letters to such organizations are worthwhile as part of your campaign to generate interest and enthusiasm before the day of the play.

To supplement the personal contact provided by visits and correspondence and to reach children who may not have been a part of groups reached directly, giveaways have more appeal than conventional advertising. Such things as balloons or suckers carrying a printed message may be made available in stores selling merchandise for children or handed out to children as they leave school at the end of the day. With some thought and imagination, perhaps the items given can have some relevance to the play beyond the printed message. Small plastic slippers, for example, might be given before a production of *Cinderella*.

The excitement of anticipation reaches its climax on the day of the play. Actors assemble two hours before curtain time to begin the process of transformation. Some begin with grease paint; others plant the first strands of crepe hair into what will become a beard; perhaps someone starts the slow process of building cotton-and-latex extensions on his nose and chin; all are caught up in the spirit of the day for which they have given six weeks of rehearsal and planning.

Preparation on the day is routine—free now of the errors that were revealed under the spotlights of dress rehearsal. Music plays in the background and the room is filled with chatter, very much like preparing for another rehearsal—until someone near a window sees the first yellow school bus and shouts, "Here they come!" That is the moment when anticipation reaches its climax and all hearts beat a little faster in the excitement of adding the final necessary ingredient—an audience.

The presence of an audience in a children's theatre carries something resembling an electric charge. Its enthusiasm is contagious. Perhaps by subliminal or extrasensory means, its presence is realized even before the actors move onstage where they can hear the buzz of conversation. The excitement felt when the first bus rolled in gives way to a sense of commitment as actors move to their places.

With actors and crew ready to begin and an audience charged with enthusiasm, what could go wrong? Well—a couple of things, maybe. That buzzing audience could be a problem if it kept on buzzing its reactions to the play, and there is always the possibility that excited youngsters will take a while to settle down so that the opening scene will have a struggle for survival.

Many children's theatres like to begin the program with some kind of greeting as a transition between audience conversation and the first line of the play—especially for the primary-level audience in which at least one third probably have had no previous experience with living theatre. It may be done by the director, by a mascot character such as "Packy," the elephant who always appears with the Children's Theatre of Racine, Wisconsin, or even by a character from the play who assumes the duties of host.

The few words before the show can narrow the gap between life experience and the theatre experience that is about to begin. Everyone is "culturally deprived" in one way or another and can be helped to a happier time in the theatre if his background is considered as you decide what can be said that will best serve his needs.

Reference to familiar storybook characters will have no meaning for children who have had no opportunity to know books. Animals or the suggestion of animals can only frighten children who have never had pets or played with animal toys. And the child of affluence may be least equipped to appreciate the living theatre if each day has brought him mass media entertainment that called for no self-discipline.

Certainly the person who welcomes the audience should not spoil the fun by preaching about behavior. With a young audience, however, there may be a need for a brief orientation to the living theatre if they are accustomed to the undisciplined audience behavior of the movie theatre and to having a volume control that can bring a TV program above the noise level of their homes.

It has been estimated that the average child has spent 4,000 hours watching television before he enters the first grade. How little he knows of the self-discipline that contributes so much to live theatre enjoyment! Reminding him that a live theatre experience is different is one way to help ensure a good time.

Knowing the audience probably will suggest still other things that need to be said or will contribute to theatre enjoyment. If the play can be related to their own experience, to things the children know, or things they have wondered about, the feeling of anticipation is heightened, and they will be all the

Original program cover designs provide another opportunity for the active play of imagination.

more ready to become involved in the experience you will share with them.

One way to bring them closer to that experience is to introduce a character or carry some prop that they will recognize when they see it in use later on the stage. Or some visual aid may be used to help explain something that must be understood. Before a performance of *Rumpelstiltskin,* for example, a ball and phonograph record were used to clarify the fantastic premise on which the setting, described as "the edge of the world," was based. Although they all knew that the world was round like a ball, enjoyment of the play would require that they *imagine* it to be round like a phonograph record.

The most important point to be considered by one who greets the audience is that *he must not talk down to them.* As directly as possible, he must communicate a spirit of welcome and his desire to help the audience enjoy the play.

The high point of realization, of course, is the play. *The play's the thing* wherein you'll catch and hold a kind of magic which defies definition or description. *Empathy, belief, involvement, excitement:* all of the favored words describing the mystique of a shared experience in the theatre take on a sharpened definition during your hour on the stage before an audience of children. If you have prepared a production appropriate to their age and interests, their unqualified honesty will reward you with a response that is electric in its spontaneity and energy.

That same honesty makes it easier to measure the success of a children's play than that of any other kind of theatre. A play that is scheduled for a series of performances can,

Young imagination travels easily to such unlikely places as this scene beside the moon, halfway between earth and sky, in Jack *and the Beanstalk.*

in fact, build upon what is learned from each new audience so as to attain a high point of excellence by the final appearance. Studying the audience to discover moments of restlessness or negative responses will suggest the need for changing the balance between talk and action, building or releasing tension at an appropriate moment, improving speech clarity, enlarging upon some character trait, or adjusting the pace of a scene. Involvement in such growth process maintains a kind of opening-night excitement through the full run of a show.

When the curtains close on each performance, one last opportunity remains for you and your audience to meet. Here begins the period of reflection, sustaining the excitement of the theatre experience. Children enjoy seeing performers close up and are excited by the nearness of one who moments before belonged in some faraway place represented by the setting onstage. Just as in the performance itself, in this meeting it is important to consider the age and level of sophistication and to continue to show the same respect for them as was evident in performance.

The comments of primary children generally indicate that they like to carry the illusion of the play into their new meeting with the players. "I don't like you" is high praise for one who demonstrated evil on stage, and "You're beautiful" is more than a personal compliment to an actress. It indicates a continuing admiration for one whose beauty was a significant factor in the play. Indeed, it is not uncommon for such statements to be made when audience members and actors meet on the street weeks after the performance.

Children at the intermediate level often are curious about how an illusion was created onstage. They are fascinated by the *differences* noted between the actor as they observe him and the character they saw on the stage. Sometimes they ask how-to-do-it questions and offer compliments such as, "I liked the way you . . ." and go on to describe something they especially enjoyed in performance or stagecraft.

To the actors, stage crew, and director of a play for children, such audience reaction sustains the excitement of the play beyond the final curtain call. It helps to reveal the nature of your involvement together and is more eloquent and rewarding than a good review in the evening paper.

That final dialogue as the audience leaves the theatre may begin the period of reflection on the play, but there is no guessing when—if ever—it will end. Two years after a production of *The Sleeping Beauty* the girl who played the title role opened the door of her home to admit dinner guests and found that their daughter was a starry-eyed admirer who could speak of nothing but the thrill of seeing "Beauty" again. More recently a group of high-school juniors expressed a determined wish to do *Greensleeves' Magic* as "our play" because they still delighted in the memory of a performance they had seen eight years before.

Between the glow of immediate responses from an enthusiastic audience leaving the theatre and the reflections that cover a span of years are other experiences—both spontaneous and planned—that stir memories of the exciting hour. Fan mail almost surely follows a play that has been attended by elementary-school classes. The letters reveal much of what kind of impression the play really made and perhaps even more of the creative involvement of the audience.

Frequently pictures will accompany fan letters and usually contain distortions of setting, costume, and characters. They help the actors and crew to realize that the true picture was not just what actors, designers, and crew placed on the stage. Their function really was to *suggest*. The memory carried home with each member of the audience was his response to the suggestion. Thus, a part of the setting involved in an emotionally stimulating scene might appear much larger by reflection than it ever was in the reality of the scene design. Or a minor character

A child and a high-school actor shared a common pleasure in reflecting on a children's theatre performance of The Elves and the Shoemaker.

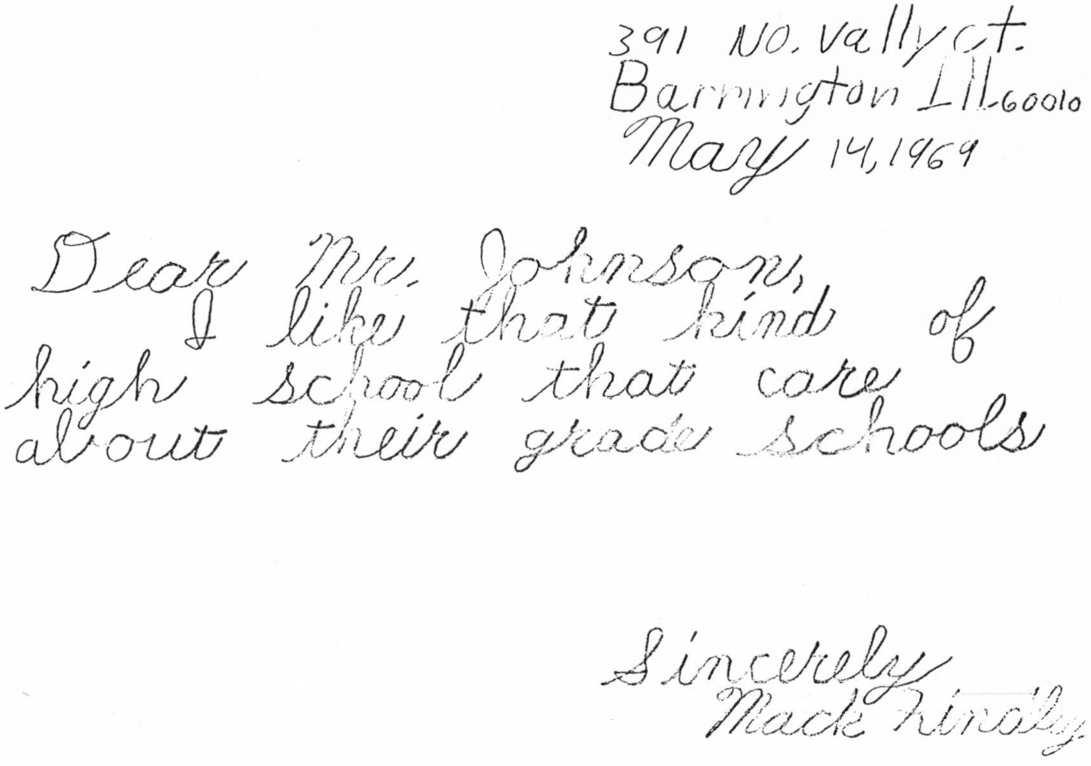

391 No. Vally ct.
Barrington Ill. 60010
May 14, 1969

Dear Mr. Johnson,
I like that kind of
high school that care
about their grade schools

Sincerely
Mack Kinaly

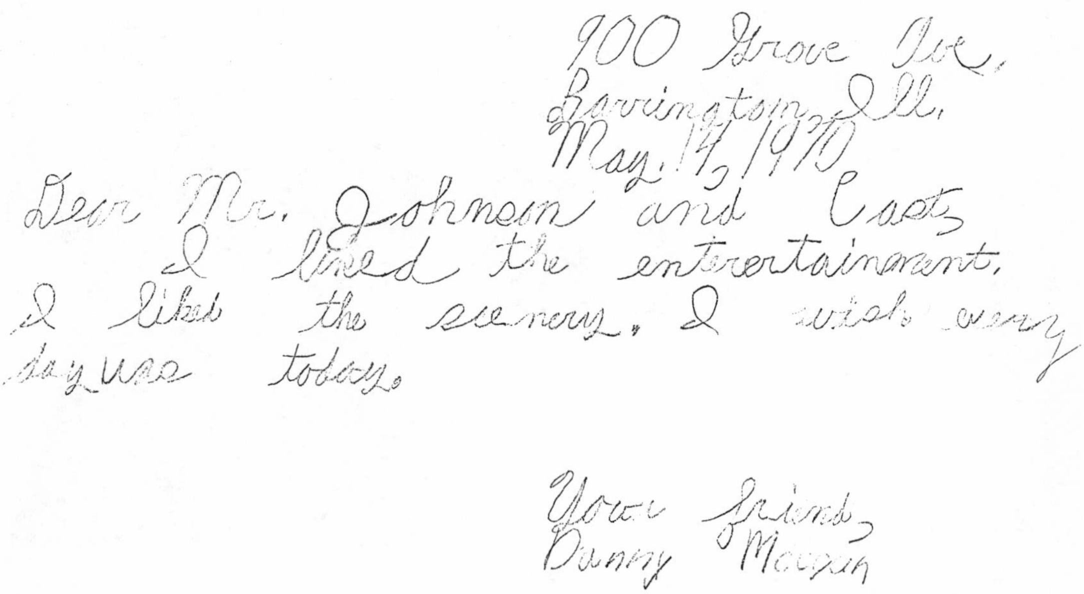

900 Grove Ave.
Barrington Ill.
May 14, 1970
Dear Mr. Johnson and Casts
I liked the entertainment.
I liked the scenery. I wish every
day was today.

Your friend,
Danny Marxin

An exciting follow-up on performance is the flood of fan mail from children who find their own unique ways of expressing enthusiasm and gratitude. Letters like these reflected the natural honesty of children and revealed to cast and crew something about the play's success.

who had successfully stimulated imagination might emerge as the dominant figure in a young artist's representation of the scene.

The letters, too, are revealing and become the subjects of much interest and pleasure as cast and crew read through them. They are thoughtful and amusing, helpful and confusing. They suggest things done well and occasionally indicate a misunderstanding. Whatever the message, they provide one more tie between performer and audience and add to the developing insight that both feeds upon and feeds good children's theatre.

In addition to fan mail that stems spontaneously from the enthusiasm of the audience and perhaps the suggestion of an equally enthusiastic teacher, some follow-up activities can be planned by your producing organization.

Backstage tours can be offered, and sometimes how-we-did-it sessions can be presented for class groups. Such meetings are especially interesting to intermediate and junior-high or middle-school classes. They are at an age when it's fun to be fooled but it's more fun to know. Knowledge can help to build more appreciative audiences for future productions.

Displays, too, can help to satisfy curiosity and stir pleasant memories of a theatre experience. They may be sent around to schools for their immediate value and then set up in the lobby to be enjoyed again when children return to your theatre for another show.

The total experience—anticipation, realization, and reflection—must be weighed if a true measure of theatre magic is to be found. Each should be exercised fully as you seek to help your theatre achieve its maximum potential in meeting the needs and satisfying the interests of both the audience and your performing group.

Chapter X

Taking a play on tour reverses the usual process of bringing the audience to the theatre. Because it is possible to build in some conveniences on home ground, getting the show on the road without them has some built-in problems. Both actors and technicians must adapt to the varied performance facilities that are likely to be encountered, and those responsible for business arrangements occasionally run into surprises, too.

Scenery for touring must be designed for portability. If it is possible to see all performance sites before a show goes to the drawing board, specific consideration can be given to their unique features as the set is planned. In general, however, touring sets should be designed so as to break down into easily portable units that will pass through an ordinary doorway and can be carried up stairs and around corners. The set should be adaptable to a variety of stage heights and capable of being expanded or compressed by adding, eliminating, or overlapping pieces, as dictated by proscenium width and stage depth.

It is relatively easy if a show calls for only a single interior setting. Children's plays rarely do, however, and some ingenuity will be required to meet the special challenges of each new show that goes on tour.

The most uncomplicated way to get two sets—with a minimum use of material—is to cover flats on both sides and decorate each side differently. A scene change can be made quickly and easily by reversing and, perhaps, rearranging them.

Another variation on flat scenery is the use of removable panels. Openings in flats may be filled with windows, doors, bookcases, or panels of varying color and design. By removing, replacing, or rearranging the units, a variety of scenic effects can be created without ever moving the basic set.

The appearance of a changed set can also be effected by mounting a decorated window shade on each flat. A new locale may then be speedily created simply by raising or lowering the shades.

An ancient device for rapid scene change is the *periaktos*. It is a three-sided structure of flat scenery. Each of the three sides is painted to represent part of a different scene, and a change of setting is made by moving each unit one third of the way around in either direction. By combining this technique with the use of removable panels and decorated window shades as indicated above, an infinite variety of scenic effects is possible.

The designer's imagination can be given much more freedom if available space and the budget will permit the use of wagons (i.e., low platforms mounted on casters on which scenic units can be mounted and moved). Trees, rock formations, steps, and platforms as well as units of flat scenery can be securely mounted on wagons and moved to offstage areas as scene changes require. While one wagon is onstage during a performance, another backstage can be reset for the next scene, permitting the quick and easy movement of heavy or bulky units and making possible the use of several settings.

If you have permission to fasten things to the floor of the stage, wagons can be mounted to move around a center post. Thus it becomes a small revolving stage and carries units that move quickly into place for two separate scenes.

Bulky units such as platforms, ramps, and steps provide problems in scene change and storage offstage, and they are equally troublesome to transport from one performance to the next. Until recently, the usual way of breaking down such units so as to occupy minimum space was to use hinged, collapsible frames of wood construction called parallels. Any stagecraft book will show how they are designed and built.

A newer and more compact approach to such construction is the use of 1″ pipes secured by fittings that may be tightened quickly with a ratchet, crescent, or hex wrench. The technique has the added advantage of making possible the design and easy construction of unusual shapes such as circular or curving stair units and large rocks of irregular shape sturdy enough to support action.

Whether or not you plan to tour a show, pipe construction offers some important advantages over the more traditional use of lumber for supporting and bracing bulky set pieces. The lack of adequate storage space is not a problem unique to the touring theatre, and at home or away, dismantled pipe units are reduced to plywood and hardware. and fittings can be reused indefinitely. Further, there is no likelihood of splitting timbers as units are dismantled, so the pipes

The size of units so constructed is limited only by the size of the stage. A huge rock or the curving stair to a castle tower can be built without difficulty or danger. Hardware is available to provide cross-bracing where it is needed.

The same kind of pipe construction can be used to build a false proscenium, designed to fit on the smallest stage to which a show will tour and, perhaps, expandable to permit a larger playing space on other stages. With such a device to focus attention on the stage, a setting of limited size will not appear to be lost in a large area such as a gymnasium or cafeteria.

The simplest kind of false proscenium is a pipe frame on which are hung a border curtain and side curtains to mask out the overhead and offstage areas. A somewhat more interesting alternative is to frame the stage with something that functions as a part of the scene design (foliage, circus banners, etc.). In that case, of course, the false proscenium is redesigned to suit each production.

Similarly, at the rear of the stage it is possible to set up a frame on which a sky drop or some other background scene is hung. Because the false proscenium limits the audience's view, such drops can be much smaller than they would have to be if no masking devices were used.

The false proscenium should be designed to support a light batten running across the front of the stage just behind the teaser or front border curtain. Again, this is simplified if pipe construction is used. The first pipe, or light batten, is intended to support a number of spotlights that serve to illuminate upstage acting areas and to create mood or other special effects through the use of color and light.

The downstage acting areas must be lighted from above the audience. If the theatre does not have a place for mounting ante-proscenium lights, pipe can be used again—this time to construct light trees that stand out in front of the stage at both right and left. Some care must be taken to mount them on a broad enough base to prevent their toppling over under the weight of the spotlights they carry. Obviously, they must be far enough to the side so as not to obstruct the audience's view of the stage.

If the theatres visited are not equipped with borderlights to illuminate the sky or other background scenic effects, floodlights with appropriate gelatin or plastic color media should be carried for that purpose. Borderlights are preferable, however, because the mixing of red, blue, and green light at various intensities can produce virtually any color one may wish. Often changes in mood

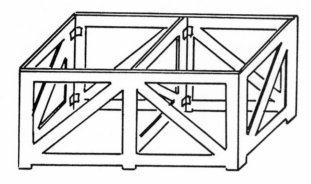

Hinged parallel framework such as this becomes a platform when topped with a loose plywood cover.

Topped with a similar cover this parallel frame becomes a ramp.

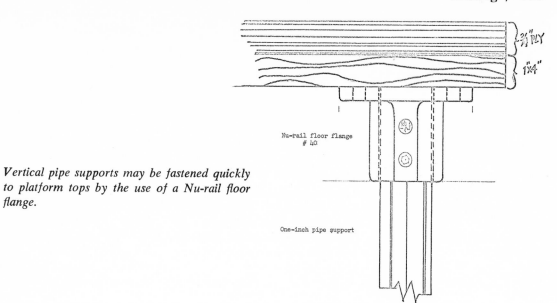

Vertical pipe supports may be fastened quickly to platform tops by the use of a Nu-rail floor flange.

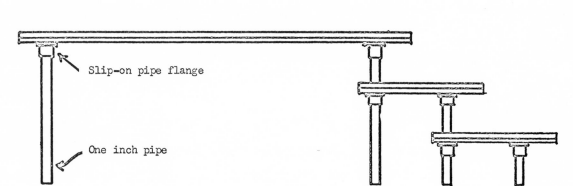

Using pipe, a platform and step unit can be assembled quickly.

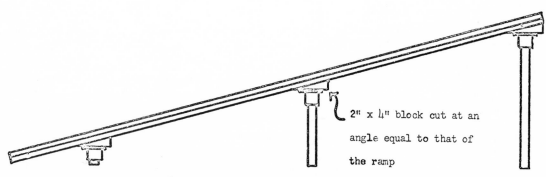

2" x 4" block cut at an angle equal to that of the ramp

Or a ramp can be similarly constructed.

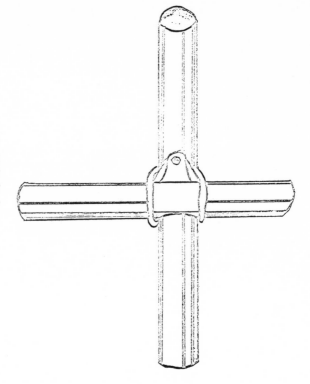

Hardware is available for easy assembly of pipe in both cross-bracing and angle-bracing for construction of the false proscenium as well as such large scenic elements as rocks and platforms. The device shown here is commercially known as the Rota-lock.

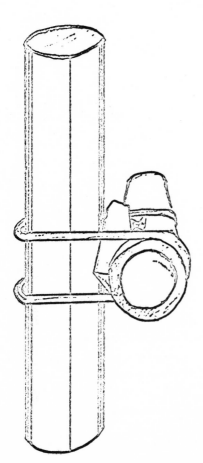

The Rota-lock is a simple device for making very secure cross connections of pipe supports.

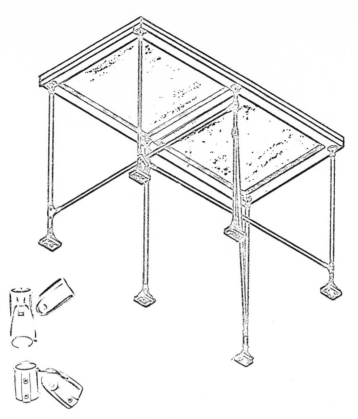

Speed-rail, Nu-rail, and Kee-Klamp are all brand names for fittings similar to those shown above and are available to serve a variety of needs. They make possible exceptionally sturdy angle-bracing for large units that must carry a lot of weight or support vigorous action. Sources for pipe hardware are listed in Appendix F.

can be effected or time of day can be suggested by a change in the sky or by washing the entire scene with a flood of color.

Lighting devices can, in fact, do more to create scenic effects than simply to paint the sky or bathe the scene with sunlight. Touring companies often find that projecting a scene cuts time, cost, and transportation difficulties. Instead of building a tree or groundrow or skyline, one can design it in miniature and project it from the rear on a translucent screen—or, if the equipment can be concealed behind onstage scenic elements, project it from the front.

A slide projector with a wide-angle lens can be used, but the most widely used and most flexible device is the Linnebach projector or something that operates on the same principle. Essential elements for such scene projection are a concentrated-filament lamp, a housing for it with no reflecting surfaces (a metal can or box painted black), and the image to be projected.

Designs for such projections often are created by trial and error, manipulating various objects before the light source until a desired effect is achieved. Twigs, branches, flowers, weeds, potted plants, wood or metal figures, and cardboard cutouts are all possible parts of a scene to be projected. Or the scene may be carefully planned and painted with transparent dyes on clear acetate or glass.

Of course, many colors can be projected through the use of dyes, but the projection of shadow images also can employ color effectively. If the screen is washed with color from floodlights, and a contrasting color is mounted over the light source, the scene appears to have been painted with light.

An overhead projector of the type employed in classrooms also can be used to

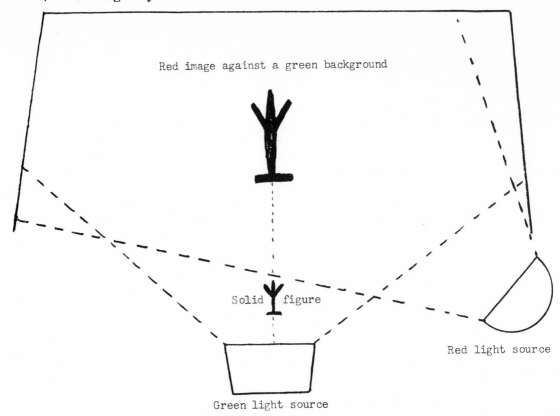

Red image against a green background

Solid figure

Red light source

Green light source

To have the enlarged shadow of an object appear red against a green background, the light source casting the shadow should be green, and an instrument of lesser intensity should be used to flood the projection area with red. The shadow image then will be the only part of the scene that is not receiving green light; therefore, it will appear red, the color cast into the area by the floodlight.

project both colored designs and shadow images. Since its lens system is designed for short-range enlargement of an image, it is ideally suited to the needs of a theatre with limited backstage space.

Whatever lighting instruments and techniques may be chosen, one essential element for their effective use is dimmer control. Most theatres have some kind of dimmer system, but you may be touring to places that are not always used as theatres. That means you probably will need portable dimmers as another item to carry.

Auto-transformer dimmers are most commonly used and may be purchased in portable units of varying size, capable of dimming from one to six circuits. In the purchase of dimmer equipment for touring, some thought must be given to its size and weight as well as to its practical use. A little shopping around will reveal a number of

dimmers that are not difficult to transport and that will function efficiently. New methods and better systems are continually being developed, so it is a good idea to shop carefully. Once you have made your selection, you will have to live with it a long time.

One other practical consideration is electrical cable. Unless the stages on which you work have built-in lighting systems, you will need a lot of it to bring all lighting instruments under dimmer control. Electrical outlets probably will be found in locations unsuited to your purposes, and you must be prepared to extend power sources to where they are needed.

So much concern for technical detail may seem to suggest that only the touring stage crew is faced with unpredictables. Not so. The actor, too, will find his assignment challenging and sometimes frustrating.

The most obvious of his problems, from

what has been said so far, is adjusting to the technical adjustments. Clearly, if the acting area is wider, narrower, deeper, or more shallow than he has known it in rehearsal and performances on home ground, he must adapt his stage business to meet the new requirements. A scene may have been prepared to include an exciting dash across a twelve-foot open space between a tree and a rock, then a leap to the top of the rock. But if a small stage requires that the tree stand beside or behind the rock and a low ceiling threatens head injury if the leap is attempted, another way of generating excitement must be improvised.

The size of the theatre also will influence performance. Both voice and body are used differently in a large house than in a small one. To reach a distant back row, action must be broader and vocal force greater than in the intimate audience relationship afforded by a small house. Acoustical eccentricities also may require that volume be increased or that an important line be delivered from a different location on the stage.

Needless to say, it is important that actors arrive early to check out the special problems imposed by each new theatre. Most desirable of all would be a rehearsal onstage —at least a rehearsal of those scenes that promise problems.

Offstage problems should be checked out early, too. Small washrooms, school classrooms, or backstage space set off by folding screens may turn out to be the only facilities for costume change and the application of stage makeup.

The actor's real concern, of course, is the children in his audience. If adjusting to the many inconveniences of touring leads to a meaningful theatre experience for them, he is likely to conclude that it was all worthwhile. To insure that happy experience, he should seek to discover as much as he can about the background of each new audience. Cultural differences must be recognized, appreciated, and played to. If the player on tour can combine the spirit of a missionary with the insight of a sociologist, he will find ways of reaching each new audience and will be richly rewarded by their response.

Much that was said in the preceding chapter about anticipating the performance applies equally well to the show preparing for a tour. Early contacts help to provide necessary insights for both you and your audience. Other preliminaries, however, are unique to the problems of touring.

Business arrangements will vary with the needs of the touring company and the nature of the audience. Ideally, the performance is subsidized by some sponsoring group, and children are invited to attend without charge. More commonly, however, some kind of profit-sharing arrangement must be made and tickets provided for advance sale. That, along with providing posters and other publicity materials, will be the responsibility of your business and publicity people.

Problems mount substantially if a tour reaches beyond commuting distance from home base. An advance agent must arrange for housing and meals, school officials must approve extended absences, families must be assured of appropriate concern for the welfare of the travelers, and the touring company itself must strive for quality in performance in spite of inevitable frustrations and fatigue. Clearly, the one-day tour has all of the advantages and a minimum of headaches.

One may hope for the day when every community will have its children's theatre, and tours will become play exchanges. During the long time of waiting, however, there is much satisfaction for those groups that tour their shows to audiences that would otherwise be denied. Only good can come of the spirit of unity that grows as an entire production team pitches in to meet the difficult challenges of going on tour.

Chapter XI

OFF AND RUNNING

Early in this century Mark Twain wrote:

It is my conviction that the children's theatre is one of the very, very great inventions of the twentieth century; and that its vast educational value—now but dimly perceived and but vaguely understood—will presently come to be recognized.

His statement was based on his observations of the Children's Educational Theatre of New York during a time when he served as its board president. It was one of the earliest ventures in children's theatre in this country other than on the professional stage and was a pace-setter for good children's theatre in many parts of the country. It lasted only from 1903 to 1908, but during that time it was clear to Mark Twain and to many others that the theatre experience could be of great benefit to children everywhere, not just to those in its settlement-house home.

Other early efforts in children's theatre were the professional success *Peter Pan* and a few others, which for a time gave promise of theatres designed specifically for the performance of children's plays. The cost was prohibitive, however, and professional children's theatre companies settled on touring as their chief means of reaching an audience.

Still another approach was initiated by the Chicago Junior League when, in 1921, it provided amateur performers to work with a professional production staff in a performance of *Alice in Wonderland*. The success of *Alice* inspired the Association of Junior Leagues of America to sponsor other local groups in amateur performances, and

children's theatre developed as a nationwide activity.

University theatre got into the act in 1925 when the Northwestern University School of Speech presented *Snow White and the Seven Dwarfs*. Two years later the Children's Theatre of Evanston was formed under the joint sponsorship of the university, the Evanston Board of Education, and the Evanston PTA. Miss Winifred Ward, whose leadership inspired the Evanston program, was destined to become a prime mover of children's theatre in educational institutions throughout the country.

At about the same time another great lady, Charlotte Chorpenning, was working a few miles down the road in Chicago's Goodman Theatre. In addition to her local production of excellent plays for children, she contributed much to the literature of children's theatre. Her plays and plays written by her students were for a long time the life's blood of American theatre for children.

Perhaps the most significant development of all came when Miss Ward became the Children's Theatre Chairman for the American Educational Theatre Association. In 1944 she gathered a committee to plan a conference that began a movement. By 1952 the Children's Theatre Conference had earned new status as a division of the American Educational Theatre Association. It had its own officers and clearly defined goals which acknowledged children's theatre to be a unique and valuable experience, deserving of a place in the lives of children everywhere.

Before long, the teen-age actor began making outstanding contributions to the chil-

This display at the 1960 White House Conference on Children and Youth brought the children's theatre idea to the attention of thousands.

dren's theatre, and high schools began to recognize it as an important part of their theatre effort—both for its significance as theatre experience and its value as a vehicle for actor training. The National Thespian Society (now the International Thespian Society) gave active support through articles in *Dramatics* as well as place on the programs of both regional and national meetings; and when the American Educational Theatre Association brought forth a division to further the aims of high-school theatre education, the Secondary School Theatre Conference found itself closely allied with the Children's Theatre Conference.

Partly through the efforts of those national organizations, the 1960 White House Conference on Children and Youth, considering ways in which this nation might provide "opportunities for children and youth to realize their full potential for a creative life in freedom and dignity," recommended that:

A. Every child should be given an opportunity to participate in creative dramatics under the guidance of qualified leadership for a basic understanding and critical appreciation of the theatre arts, and as an adjunct to constructive learning.

B. Young people should be given an opportunity to participate in dramatic production under direction of qualified leaders to acquire the emotional and intellectual disciplines inherent in the theatre arts.

The recommendations were an impetus to activity, and soon after the White House Conference a government publication, *Drama with and for Children,* appeared. More recently funds from federal and other sources have made possible a number of projects that have touched the lives of many young people directly.

Some of the projects are small and involve the performance of amateur groups for local audiences. Others result from the combined efforts of the Office of Economic Opportunity, the National Endowment for the Arts, and private foundations to bring professional performing groups to large audiences of young people. Some 41,000 Rhode Island students are served by the Trinity Square Repertory Company of Providence, and the Repertory Theatre of New Orleans brings live drama to an audience of 42,000. The Arena Stage in Washington, D.C., has organized Living Stage '69 to bring improvisational theatre to children. Indian children and teachers are offered creative drama and puppetry by the Indian Community Action Project in New Mexico. Project TRY (Theatre Resources for Youth) in New Hampshire, Project CREATE in Connecticut, Upward Bound in Arizona, the Living Arts Program in Dayton, Ohio, and many others throughout the country are demonstrating that the arts in general and theatre in particular can work marvelous changes in the attitudes and interests of children and youth.

One of the most significant recent developments has been the organizing of an International Association of Theatre for Children and Young People. Through this organization (commonly called ASSITEJ, an abbreviation of its French name), people of differing political ideologies meet to share a common enthusiasm for theatre and a common desire to enrich the lives of children through memorable theatre experiences.

In asking Congress for funds to support the National Endowment for the Arts and Humanities, the President of the United States has said, "The arts have the rare capacity to help heal divisions among our own people and to vault some of the barriers that divide the world." That miracle is not the exclusive province of government projects, nor can it be attained by them alone. It is for us—all of us who can bring the theatre experience to children—to meet our audience and strive with them to attain our full measure of humanity.

THE IMPORTANCE OF BEING HUMAN

Memorable is a word we tend to reserve for some very special things. As we reflect on times past, we single out certain experiences as being memorable. That is, we recognize that they are in a special category that seems to deny the possibility of forgetting. To be memorable, an experience must be important in a very personal way. We must feel or be involved in *doing* something, and that involvement must generate excitement.

The exciting, memory-building side of life is unique to *human* experience. Only human beings can recall, verbalize, and build upon memories. Without that uniquely human ability, nothing creative could occur. Without it, there could be no art. And without art, human experience would be less memorable—less human.

That is especially true in a technological age when survival, vocational success, and even a kind of progress seem assured for one who is locked into the established system—with little or no challenge to his creative energies, little or no need to be a unique human being.

Long ago, as children grew up in a land where there was room to expand and survival depended upon the exercise of human ingenuity, they found a very proper soil in which imagination might grow and blossom. It was, in fact, this flowering imagination that produced inventions and techniques which now invite man to vegetate—perhaps to evolve a life form in which the imagination is no more functional than the appendix.

The problem is one of reduced necessity for each person to dream his own dream and greater temptation for him to be served by the product of someone else's inventive mind. As we enjoy the security granted by efficient approaches to organizing, maintaining, and repairing both our machines and ourselves, we are in danger of allowing our human resources to deteriorate into something less human.

Of course, the worth of the individual is recognized in our political system and is protected by our Constitution. But human worth cannot be maintained merely because it has been legislated and documented. Human values must be experienced and realized if they are to exist in the lives of people, not just in their books.

Throughout the history of civilized man, the arts in general and the theatre in particular have provided human beings with the means of sharing what their imaginations could envision as they sought to discover meaning in their lives. The most fundamental human questions have centered around man's awareness of his own magnificence. Realizing his worth, he has sought to understand it; and in his quest, he has learned to realize more fully his kinship with all other human beings.

There never has been a time in history when the humanizing effect of the theatre experience was more urgently needed. We have come to depend more upon machines than upon ourselves for success and survival, and the crowding of our planet has led us to the habit of classification, considering people in bulk lots rather than as unique individuals. Schools have fallen into the simple expedient of lumping students into groups labeled *accelerated, high ability, high average, average, low average, slow learner,* etc. An entire age group has been labeled *teen-ager.* All of those along with various racial, ethnic, economic, geographic, educational, and occupational groups often are regarded as though the characteristics held in common are of greater consequence than those qualities that make each individual unique.

When to that penchant for easy classification we add the convenience and efficiency of computer programming, we can readily recognize the dehumanizing influence of modern institutions as they become increasingly oriented to modern technology. At such a time experiences that elevate and dignify the human spirit are essential balancing forces.

Reaction to the dehumanizing forces may be seen in many places. Some seek *escape* by finding their "kicks" in alcohol, some in drugs, some in entertainment—anything that will help them "turn on" and make it possible to "tune out" the pressures that make up each day's experience. Others try to fight back, to break out of the mold in which the system has cast them, and the result is violence as seen in rioting and a wide range of criminal behaviors—or it may be in the exercise of imagination through some kind of creative activity.

The great need is to find a way *in* to those experiences that are uniquely human, not a way of escaping those that are inevitably imposed by an advancing technology.

The generation gap that seems of concern to so many people really is not so much a gap between generations as it is a gap between contrasting attitudes toward change. Those who recognize that changing times always will introduce new roles to play will change with the times. The gap between them and those who remain rigidly set in the roles learned a generation before will be very real indeed.

Learning to adapt to new roles is the business of the theatre. It provides a vital experience in the important business of closing the attitude gap and nourishing our ailing humanity. Those who would live well tomorrow must cultivate imagination today.

There is excitement in anticipating a new role, as any actor knows. There is excitement, too, in identifying with the experiences of others—empathizing as we do in the theatre—and that feeling of identity with our fellow humans is essential if the human spirit is to survive current dehumanizing influences. That is the mission of the theatre in our time.

A striking example of that mission and the power of theatre to work its wonders in rehabilitation may be seen in the Theatre of the Forgotten, a professional troupe that tours the prisons of New York, performing for and with the prisoners. The miracle of involvement has changed the lives of many who were reached by Akila Couloumbis, Beverly Rich, and their company of players. How much more wonderful it might have been if the humanizing influence of the theatre had been a part of their lives from the beginning.

This is the mission of the children's theatre: It is the Theatre of the Remembered. It can reach its audience at a time when it is most receptive and most excited by the promise of change, when attitudes and behaviors are not set, when new role identification is a part of normal play activity.

John E. Anderson, Director of the Child Welfare Foundation, University of Minnesota, has indicated that material presented to children in dramatic form carries over into their fantasy and play. Although their skill at recall is not as great as that of adolescents and adults, they retain more of what was originally recalled than do older persons. They play out their dramatic experiences both physically and in mental reflection. "Much of the stimulating value of an experience," he said, "arises out of the extent of this carry-over into subsequent relations and practices. Other things being equal, the better performance gains its meaning, not from what happens during its presentation, but from what happens later."

The better performance, then, is one that plants suggestion rather than carefully disclosing so much that nothing is left to be imagined. With the power of suggestion at work, the theatre experience can set off a continuing creative process.

Dr. Anderson has warned against allowing the attitude gap to influence the content of children's theatre. Those who would provide a theatre experience for children, he said, should "project themselves back into earlier levels and see again the world they saw as children." Research has shown that when children have equal opportunity to choose between good and poor materials, they will choose the better. But the way to provide better children's theatre is to improve it from the children's point of view—to make it exciting and appealing in *their* terms.

Without aesthetic involvement, it is only too easy for children to grow to adult life that does not identify readily with the world of people and for many to feel isolated or remote from the human concerns that relate man to his fellows. If people are to live well in this new age, they must hold on to their humanness.

The computer spirit is not a substitute for the human spirit but, rather, is a great liberator of man, permitting him to indulge more fully in those memorable experiences that can give meaning and value to his humanity. Those experiences belong to every age level and can exist significantly in the children's theatre.

Far from being the slave of modern technology, each player in your theatre and each member of your audience can become a creative power, sensing ever more fully the excitement of being human and realizing ever more completely the essential truths that bring joy to the theatre experience and make him one with his fellow man.

A PRODUCTION CALENDAR

One good way to avoid the last-minute jitters is to consider the performance date as only one of a series of deadlines. If each is met in turn, nothing is left to pile up at the finish. Only thus can everyone from director to usher enjoy the excitement of theatre, free from the anxiety of "getting the show on the road."

The following breakdown of responsibilities assumes a six-week preparation period. If all members of the leadership team stay on schedule, scenery, lights, properties, costumes, special effects, makeup, play, and audience will all be ready at the same time.

BUSINESS MANAGER

Before the first week:

1. Complete all arrangements for scheduling rehearsal hall, stage shop, and theatre.
2. Obtain scripts and the publisher's permission to produce the play.
3. Complete all touring arrangements.
4. Investigate printing costs for tickets, programs, and posters.

First week:

1. Submit ticket copy to the printer.
2. Arrange with a local merchant to have space for selling tickets and/or making seat reservations.

Second week:

1. Obtain poster designs, program cover designs, and copy for any printed matter to be used in publicity from the publicity chairman.
2. Order engravings if necessary and submit all materials to the printer.

Third week:

1. Obtain a cast list and the names of all active committee workers and prepare copy for a dummy program.
2. Post the dummy program so that all concerned may make corrections in spelling and suggest additions or deletions.
3. If the program will carry advertising, obtain copy from all participating merchants.
4. Submit the corrected dummy program and all advertising copy to the printer.
5. Place tickets in numbered packets and check them out to all who will participate in the advance sale. Maintain a careful record of ticket distribution.

Fourth week:

1. Pay royalties for all scheduled performances.
2. Continue checking out advance sale tickets and keep a careful record of all money turned in by salesmen.
3. Schedule salesmen for duty selling tickets and/or reserving seats in some local place of business each day until the theatre box office is open.

Fifth week:

1. Schedule people for box-office duty.
2. Continue careful supervision of the advance sale.

Sixth week:

1. Set up all necessary supplies for box-office ticket sale and/or seat reservation.
2. Obtain an adequate supply of change for the box office.

3. Get programs from the printer and turn them over to the House Manager.
4. Collect all money and advance sale tickets that have not been sold.
5. Supervise the box-office sale and maintain a careful accounting of all funds.

PUBLICITY COMMITTEE

Before the first week:

1. Read the play and interview the director and technical director to determine items of special interest to a prospective audience.
2. Prepare a news release announcing the choice of play and plans being made for its production.

First week:

1. Reread the play and visit at least one rehearsal.
2. Meet in committee to plan special promotional activities. Assign responsibility for poster and program designs as well as other art work required by the committee's plan for promotion of the play.
3. Place orders for any materials needed in the publicity campaign.
4. Get permission from school authorities, police, and any concerned merchants for the display of publicity materials.
5. Prepare a news release announcing the cast and presenting a progress report.

Second week:

1. Submit poster and program designs to the director for approval and decide on a method of poster production.
2. Set up a plan for ticket distribution and organize necessary crews to make up packets and maintain records.
3. Prepare a news release announcing the appointment of committees.

Third week:

1. Plan a coloring book and/or other publicity materials to be distributed in elementary schools.
2. Submit rehearsal pictures to nearby newspapers.
3. Prepare a news release reviewing the progress of rehearsals.

Fourth week:

1. Complete art work and stencils for the coloring book and/or other handouts.
2. Submit pictures of crews and committees at work to nearby newspapers.
3. Distribute posters for display in schools and store windows.
4. Arrange for a sound truck to be used in publicizing the play on the days of performance.
5. Prepare a news release reviewing the progress of committees and crews.

Fifth week:

1. Arrange for ticket distribution through local schools and selected merchants.
2. Submit recent rehearsal pictures to nearby newspapers.
3. Secure permission for cast members in costume to appear in elementary-school classes and organize groups for those appearances.
4. Assemble coloring books.
5. Send complimentary tickets and letters of invitation to local teachers, Scoutmasters, leaders of church organizations, etc.
6. Submit copy for public service announcements to nearby radio stations.
7. Prepare a news release featuring something unusual about the production or some technical problem that has been solved in an interesting or unique manner.

Sixth week:

1. Submit dress-rehearsal pictures for publication in nearby newspapers.
2. Take costumed cast members to local schools for previously arranged appearances in elementary-school classes.
3. Deliver coloring books and other handouts to elementary schools.
4. Prepare a news release reviewing performance dates, relating cast members to high points in the plot, and repeating significant information reported earlier about leadership roles played by various members of the group.
5. On performance dates, drive a sound truck through areas from which the play is most likely to draw its audience.

Seventh week:

1. Collect all publicity materials appearing in public places.
2. Write thank-you notes to individuals and organizations that helped in promotion of the play.
3. Submit all bills to the business manager.

PHOTOGRAPHER

First week:

1. Read the play and visit at least one rehearsal.
2. Discuss photographic needs with the publicity chairman and the director.

Second week:

1. Take pictures of scenes in rehearsal.
2. Photograph various crews and committees at work.

Third week:

1. Print pictures, enlarging those that appear to be interesting as a record of the play-production process.
2. Identify the people who appear in the selected photographs and turn them over to the publicity chairman.
3. Continue photographing both cast and crews, being especially careful to get newsworthy pictures of crews and committees at work.

Fourth week:

1. Print pictures, enlarging the most interesting.
2. Identify the people appearing in the enlarged photographs and turn them over to the publicity chairman.
3. Continue photographing both cast and crews. If possible, arrange for some rehearsal shots in costume.

Fifth week:

1. Print pictures, enlarging the most interesting.
2. Identify people in the enlarged photographs and turn them over to the publicity chairman.
3. Photograph cast and crews in rehearsal onstage, capturing scenic elements and other items of technical interest.

Sixth week:

1. Print pictures, enlarging the most interesting.
2. Turn them over to the publicity chairman, with all people appearing in the pictures identified.
3. Photograph cast appearances in elementary schools.
4. Photograph both cast and crews in dress rehearsals.
5. Print and enlarge the latter for last-minute publicity use and for lobby display.

STAGE MANAGER

First week:

1. Read the play.
2. Confer with the scene designer, technical director, and director about the design concept and special technical needs and problems.
3. Meet with all crew heads to consider how they will function in meeting those needs and problems.

Second week:

1. Coordinate all crew activities to ensure a unified approach to the director's and scene designer's concept of the show.
2. Confer with lighting, properties, and special-effects chairmen on the plotting of cues.

Third week:

1. Continue supervision of crews to ensure strict adherence to the time schedule.
2. Work with the lighting, properties, and special-effects chairmen in the preparation of cue sheets. Check all details with the technical director and director.

Fourth week:

1. Number all cues in the prompt book and anticipate each with a WARN cue.
2. Be sure that all areas where crews will function during the show are clean, uncluttered, and well organized.
3. Plan and supervise all crew rehearsals.

Fifth week:

1. Supervise all crew functions during technical rehearsals.

2. Observe all technical effects and advise necessary changes in the timing and content of technical cues.

Sixth week:

1. For final technical rehearsals, dress rehearsals, and performances, check on the function of all technical equipment and the location of all stage properties at least one hour before curtain time.
2. Assume complete responsibility for all onstage activity during rehearsals and performances.
3. Be certain that all properties, actors, and running crew are in place and ready before cueing the start of an act or scene.

Seventh week:

1. Supervise all crews in strike and cleanup activities.
2. Be certain that all equipment is put away, all borrowed property returned, and work areas left clean and in good order.

SCENERY CREW

First week:

1. Read the play.
2. Study the scene design and confer with the stage manager to review technical problems and determine what scenic elements will be needed to complete the setting.
3. Check the inventory for available scenic elements.
4. Set up a job chart assigning necessary tasks to meet the need for new construction.
5. Order all materials needed for new construction.

Second week:

1. Work on new construction.
2. Re-cover old flats where necessary and complete other needed repairs.
3. Batten or hinge and dutchman all places where flats are joined.
4. Begin sizing of new flats and laying in base colors on all scenery.

Third week:

1. Complete all new construction
2. Complete sizing and basic painting.
3. Mount scenery onstage.
4. Begin scenic art work.

Fourth week:

1. Continue scenic art work.
2. Clean up the backstage area and put away all construction equipment.
3. Assign specific tasks for all scene changes and rehearse.

Fifth week:

1. Complete scenic art work.
2. Rehearse all crew functions during the regular cast rehearsals.

Sixth week:

1. Work for maximum efficiency in scene changes during technical and dress rehearsals, carefully timing all movements.
2. Clean carefully both onstage and backstage.
3. Apply a final coat of paint to steps and platforms that have been soiled in rehearsal.
4. Run carefully timed scene changes during all performances.

Seventh week:

1. Strike sets and clean the stage area.
2. Dismantle all units not to be saved, and store reusable lumber and hardware.
3. Add new scenic elements being stored to the inventory list.
4. Clean the stage shop.

LIGHTING CREW

First week:

1. Read the play and note any lighting effects specifically called for by the playwright.
2. Make a list of other moments in the play when you think unusual lighting should be employed.
3. Check your findings with the director, technical director, and stage manager, and consider their application within the limitations and requirements of the design concept.

Second week:

1. Check the inventory of gelatin and other color media and order whatever additional supplies are needed.
2. Attend rehearsals and note positions of the actors in scenes where lighting changes seem desirable.
3. Using that information as the basis for discussion and planning, confer with the stage manager and technical director and begin making a light plot.

Third week:

1. Using a scale drawing of the stage floor plan, sketch in the positions of lighting instruments and the areas of light projected, showing their relationship to the stage setting.
2. Prepare a schedule of specific tasks for crew members.
3. Focus all lighting instruments.
4. Prepare cue sheets.

Fourth week:

1. Make a careful check of all lighting instruments for location, focus, and direction.
2. Install appropriate color media on all lighting instruments.
3. Rehearse lighting cues with the stage manager.

Fifth week:

1. Put away all equipment that will not be used in the show.
2. Rehearse cues during the cast rehearsals and confer with the stage manager and technical director about possible changes in location, timing, color, or intensity.

Sixth week:

1. Check direction and focus of all lighting instruments before each rehearsal and performance.
2. Adjust cue sheets to reveal any changes in timing or intensity that have been approved by the technical director.
3. During performances adhere strictly to the final decisions on timing and intensity.

Seventh week:

1. Strike all instruments mounted specifically for the show.
2. Return all equipment to its proper place for storage.

PROPERTIES CREW

First week:

1. Read the play and consider its properties requirements.
2. Confer with the stage manager and technical director in setting up a list of needed properties that will be consistent with the design concept.
3. Check the props inventory to determine what is available and what must be built or borrowed.
4. Assign specific tasks in design, construction, and procurement of properties.

Second week:

1. Complete designs for new properties to be constructed.
2. Work on construction of new props.
3. Confer with the stage manager on the setting up of a properties plot.

Third week:

1. Complete the properties plot.
2. Assign specific responsibilities to the running crew.
3. Continue work on construction.

Fourth week:

1. Provide all hand props at rehearsals.
2. Set up backstage props tables and assign responsibilities for careful control of prop locations.
3. Complete all newly constructed properties.

Fifth week:

1. Provide all properties for all rehearsals.
2. Work to develop maximum efficiency in striking and setting props during scene changes.

Sixth week:

1. Check location of properties at least one hour before each rehearsal and performance.

2. Secure all properties after each rehearsal and performance.

Seventh week:

1. Inspect all properties for possible damage.
2. Return all borrowed properties and place others in storage.
3. Add newly constructed properties to the props inventory.

SPECIAL-EFFECTS CREW

First week:

1. Read the play and prepare a list of special effects that will be needed.
2. Check the inventory of recorded sounds and equipment needed for those effects.
3. Assign tasks to those who will make needed recordings and effects equipment to be operated during the show.

Second week:

1. Submit the list of special effects to the director and technical director for approval.
2. Prepare cue sheets.
3. Order whatever materials are needed to prepare special effects.
4. Select recorded intermission music and submit choices to the director for approval.

Third week:

1. Complete all recordings and other effects.
2. Separate all tape-recorded sound and music cues with cue tape.
3. Confer with the technical director, director, and stage manager to settle all remaining questions about cues.
4. Make final adjustments on cue sheets.

Fourth week:

1. Assign specific cues to crew members.
2. Set up all equipment that will be used for special effects.
3. Rehearse with the technical director and stage manager.

Fifth week:

1. Make a daily check of equipment to be sure everything works properly.
2. Rehearse cues during cast rehearsals.

Sixth week:

1. Check all equipment at least one hour before dress rehearsals and performances.
2. Run cues during rehearsals and performances.

Seventh week:

1. Return special-effects equipment and tape recordings to storage.
2. Add new sound cues and equipment to the special-effects inventory.

COSTUME CREW

First week:

1. Read the play and determine costume needs.
2. Assign costume designs.
3. Take measurements of all cast members.

Second week:

1. Make a color chart with all costume colors appearing in each scene.
2. Discuss the chart with both the director and technical director and make necessary changes.
3. Confer with the director and technical director in making final decisions about costume designs.
4. Decide which costumes must be made from new materials and which can be found in the wardrobe, borrowed, or made from existing materials.
5. Order material necessary for new costumes.
6. Assign specific tasks to all costume crew members.

Third week:

1. Schedule fittings for costumes currently available.
2. Continue work on cutting and sewing of new costumes.

Fourth week:

1. Continue work on new costumes.
2. Schedule fittings for all completed costumes.

Fifth week:

1. Complete all costumes and see that they are clean and pressed.
2. Complete fittings for all costumes.

Sixth week:

1. Deliver costumes to the dressing rooms at least two hours before curtain time on dress rehearsal and performance dates.
2. See that costumes are pressed and properly cared for after each rehearsal and performance.

Seventh week:

1. Return all borrowed costumes clean and in good condition.
2. See that all other costumes are cleaned, pressed, and added to the wardrobe.

Makeup Crew

First week:

1. Read the play to determine makeup needs.
2. Take inventory of makeup supplies.
3. Discuss makeup needs with the director and technical director and order necessary supplies.
4. Attend at least one rehearsal as preparation for makeup crew discussion of characters.

Second week:

1. Discuss characters and makeup needs.
2. Assign preliminary sketches and makeup plans.

Third week:

1. On the basis of sketches and plans submitted, assign duties to the makeup crew.
2. Practice the techniques necessary to carrying out plans.

Fourth and fifth weeks:

1. Continue practice.
2. Invite criticism and guidance from the director and technical director.

Sixth week:

1. Report for makeup two hours before curtain time.
2. Do complete makeups for all rehearsals and performances.
3. Keep at least one person backstage during performances to touch up makeup and handle unexpected emergencies.
4. Leave the makeup room clean and uncluttered after each rehearsal and performance.

AUDITION FORMS

Since an audition is an attempt to see potential players in comparison with one another as they relate to the roles they may play, any form that is used should provide the director with the information he needs to reflect on each player's attributes and to continue comparing once the audition has been completed. Further, it should serve as a reminder on matters of previous experience and training or scheduling difficulties to be encountered during rehearsals that might influence the final decision to cast or not to cast.

It is possible to develop an elaborate check list of things to look for during the audition, but this may provide such a busywork assignment for the director that he cannot give full

AUDITION INFORMATION

Name . . . .

Address . . . . Phone . . . .

Height . . . . Hair Color . . . . Age . . . .

If you have had previous acting experience, list the parts:

Do you have other useful talents or skills? (singing, dancing, fencing, tumbling, juggling, magic)

Are there other obligations (school, church, job) that will occupy a significant part of your time during the rehearsal period? . . . . List any previous commitments that will cause you to miss a rehearsal. *This is the only way in which you may arrange to be absent.*

List the roles you intend to try for *in the order of preference.*

1.

2.

3.

4.

5.

attention to the performer. To avoid that, you may prefer to use only a sheet or card on which only a name appears, adding relevant information during the audition.

The preceding form contains spaces for information that can be given by the reader before his audition and allows space for a list of characters read followed by space for the director's notes. It is a compromise between the extremes of a detailed check list and a blank sheet of paper and is intended for use in the first screening.

The "Audition Information" sheet may be used for keeping a record of individual readings of lines selected by either the reader or the director or of improvised monologues based on scenes in the play. If a second screening seems necessary before going into final auditions, the same sheet may continue to serve.

For final auditions, however, it may seem desirable to see potential players interacting in brief scenes. Choices may be further aided if the director can get some insight into the actors' means of preparation for roles.

A quick look at how each actor regards his character both objectively and subjectively may be gained if he is asked to prepare a scene with one or two others and to make some judgment of his character's speech, movement, and motivation. To judge speech and movement, he considers the character objectively and attempts to create a simile to suggest each. (He moves like a strutting rooster; she sounds like the ceaseless chatter of an air hammer.) Then he

SCENE FOR FINAL AUDITION

Two or three people who will perform together in final audition should prepare this form together. Each is asked to consider his character both objectively, in terms of speech and movement, and subjectively, in terms of motivation. The similes called for are not limited to observable human characteristics. You may find some likeness in your character to an animal or some inanimate object.

Character   *Performer*

1. _____   _____

2. _____   _____

3. _____   _____

1. _____ moves like:

   He sounds like:

   In this scene he wants:

2. _____ moves like:

   He sounds like:

   In this scene he wants:

3. _____ moves like:

   He sounds like:

   In this scene he wants:

Comments

relates subjectively to the scene and defines the principal motivation or want of his character.

The validity of those judgments is tested in the final audition when scenes involving two or three characters are performed. The real test, of course, is the relevance of the character as it relates to the play, not as it relates to information contrived for an audition form. Ideas written down are merely a step toward greater perception of the role in performance.

The preceding form is useful in developing the kind of final audition indicated here. It may be used with scenes selected either by the director or by the participants.

THE MULTI-CAST SHOW

Your approach to multiple casting will depend upon three variables: (1) the availability of more than one actor or actress who can perform effectively in each role, (2) the number of capable directors available, and (3) suitable spaces for simultaneous rehearsals and/or sufficient time in each rehearsal day to permit scheduling more than one cast onstage in a single rehearsal area. The following approaches deserve consideration.

TWO CASTS—TWO DIRECTORS

The simplest arrangement, assuming the availability of necessary talents and spaces, is to operate with two or more casts independent of each other—as though each were in its own theatre. Under that arrangement, rehearsals follow the same kind of schedule as with a single cast.

Special requirements

1. The directors must agree on a common style as reflected in stage decor and costuming.
2. Blocking must be sufficiently similar to permit use of the same properties and the same placement of lighting instruments.
3. Frequent conferences of directors are required to ensure agreement on technical details and rehearsal schedules.
4. Preferably only *one* director is responsible for liaison with technical crews. (Nothing is more demoralizing to a crew than to be caught in the middle of a disagreement between directors—incurring the wrath of one for following the instructions of the other.)
5. Duplicate costumes must be available if actors appearing in the same role are not the same size.

Advantages

1. More players have an opportunity to perform.
2. In the event of illness or accident of a player, a well-qualified performer can step in.
3. The cost is less than in two independent productions with separate technical expenses and separate opening-night royalties.
4. Performers have the opportunity of attending the show and identifying with the audience as well as gaining deeper insights into their own roles by observing other actors' interpretations.
5. The comparatively unrewarding "understudy" assignment is eliminated.
6. The audiences may be larger because of a personal interest in seeing individual performances and in repeat attendance so as to compare interpretations of both casts.

Disadvantages

1. Players may develop a competitive spirit —regarding the goal of being *better* than the other actors as being more exciting than the development of believable characters and communication of the playwright's idea. Jealousies generated by such an attitude can seriously deter the creative process.
2. Directors may find necessary areas of agreement difficult to attain.

TWO CASTS—ONE DIRECTOR AND ONE ASSISTANT DIRECTOR

Similar to the first plan is one in which two separate casts function independently but with the same director. Under this arrangement each cast rehearses alternately under the supervision

136

of a director and an assistant director. The rehearsal schedules are no different from the previous plan, but there is a rotating leadership.

Special requirements

1. The assistant director must understand thoroughly the director's concept of the play and be capable of interpreting it in a manner consistent with that of the director.
2. The director and assistant director must confer regularly, comparing notes on the development of both casts in rehearsal.
3. The assistant director must understand and be fully informed of the developing plans for the technical aspects of the production.
4. Duplicate costumes may be required as in the first plan.

Advantages

1. Both casts develop under a single and unified concept of direction, free of the disagreements that may be reflected as two directors attempt to compromise their differences or disagreements.
2. This plan retains the artistic and financial advantages of the first plan.

Disadvantages

1. Both casts are without the immediate presence of their director for half of their rehearsals.
2. This plan carries the same disadvantage of competitive spirit with the resulting potential for destructive jealousies.

One Principal Cast—Second Cast of Understudies

In most instances this is advertised and performed as a one-cast show. A second-string team of players remains in the background, perhaps playing bit parts, ready to step into major roles if an emergency should arise.

One variation is to schedule an understudies' performance, possibly a special matinee, to encourage understudies to devote the time necessary to develop competence.

Special requirements

1. Understudies must attend rehearsals regularly, even if only to observe, and must be available to step in if a regular cast member is absent.
2. An assistant director must be available to work with understudies at times other than the regular rehearsal periods.
3. If understudies cannot wear costumes of their counterparts in the regular cast, additional costumes should be available for possible understudy performance.

Advantages

1. In the event of illness or accident involving a principal player, someone is available to take his place.
2. It is not necessary to provide the space and give the time required for a full double rehearsal schedule.
3. The understudies gain experience that contributes to their training for future roles.
4. The size of the understudy cast can be adjusted to correspond with available talent, limited to major roles or extended to the entire cast.

Disadvantages

1. The understudy finds much less to motivate careful preparation since he sees only a remote possibility of replacing the actor whose role he is studying.
2. Even if a special understudy performance is scheduled, the players may smart under the "second-rate" status that the understudy label implies.
3. Limited opportunity to rehearse may cause the understudy to perform below the level of his true ability.

Rotation Casting

A somewhat more complex approach to double casting is the development of a schedule that involves a continuing change of actor-character relationships. Each role is played by two actors, but they are rearranged through rehearsals and performances scheduled to provide no two consecutive meetings of identical casts. When a cast in which he does not have a major role is working, the actor attends rehearsals as an observer and/or a performer in a minor role.

If the play will run for four or more performances, the rotation can be designed to establish four separate sets of actor-character relationships even though there are, in fact, only two actors for each role.

Assuming that there are eight characters in a play, a simple double-casting arrangement might show them as:

Role	Cast 1	Cast 2
Miss A.	Joanne	Claire
Mr. B.	Marshall	John
Miss C.	Colleen	Debbie
Mr. D.	Ted	Chip
Miss E.	Becky	Mary
Mr. F.	Peter	Richard
Miss G.	Pam	Carey
Mr. H.	Andy	Art

The following chart shows how the same players might appear in a four-cast rotation:

Role	Cast 1	Cast 2	Cast 3	Cast 4
Miss A.	Joanne	Joanne	Claire	Claire
Mr. B.	Marshall	John	John	Marshall
Miss C.	Debbie	Colleen	Debbie	Colleen
Mr. D.	Ted	Ted	Chip	Chip
Miss E.	Becky	Mary	Mary	Becky
Mr. F.	Peter	Richard	Peter	Richard
Miss G.	Pam	Carey	Carey	Pam
Mr. H.	Andy	Andy	Art	Art

Special requirements

1. The full double cast must attend all rehearsals, permitting the director to rotate actors during any scene that he believes can be more meaningfully developed through on-the-spot rotation of one or more players.
2. All actors must recognize the importance of observation, seeking to empathize as they witness the development of other actors in the roles they will play.
3. Special care must be taken to ensure equal rehearsal time for all casts.

Advantages

1. All of the practical advantages of a double cast are retained.
2. It is possible to double cast all or only a few selected major roles.
3. No one has cause to feel that he is a "second class" actor by being identified as an understudy.
4. The continuing interchange of players keeps each cast from developing a special identity and a feeling of competition with and/or jealousy of other casts.
5. The feeling of unity embracing all casts stimulates loyalty to the play and to the purpose it seeks to accomplish in meeting a child audience.
6. The actors gain a broader experience as they interact with other players in a flexible cast arrangement, contributing something of value to their growth in the art of theatre.

Disadvantages

1. If two actors in the same role have significantly different interpretations, they may have difficulty adjusting to cooperative rehearsal techniques and/or create confusion among actors who perform with them.
2. Rehearsals may be longer than if only a single cast were being prepared for performance. (Since children's plays usually are comparatively short, however, the total time required probably will be no longer than conventional preparation of a single cast for adult theatre.)

CONCLUSION

The weight of evidence in this presentation seems to favor the use of rotation casting. Probably no one approach can be called the best, however, for all groups and all occasions. Weighing the advantages and disadvantages of each will suggest the method most likely to serve a given play most effectively.

REHEARSAL SCHEDULES

Staying on schedule is vital to the successful development of a play in rehearsal. Failure to meet early deadlines leads to inevitable rushing through the maturation process that a play must experience as it grows through its final weeks of preparation. There must be a time of growing comfortable with the habits of speech and movement that belong to each moment in the play if the events that occur onstage in performance are to be believed by the audience.

The following schedules are for six-week preparation periods with four rehearsals each week. The first assumes a single cast or two casts under separate directors, each independent of the other in rehearsal.

fourth week. Some memorization occurs during rehearsals, but additional study time will be necessary to meet the deadline on each act. Such study is most productive when it is accompanied by action that simulates that of rehearsal as nearly as possible.

Throughout the fifth and sixth weeks rehearsals should proceed without interruption, the director taking notes on those things he wishes to see improved or corrected. The procedure permits a feeling of unity to build so that dress rehearsals in the sixth week can have the same smoothness as the opening performance.

Following this plan, each *cast* has five or six

REHEARSAL SCHEDULE

Single Cast

	Monday	Tuesday	Wednesday	Thursday
First Week	Acts I–II–III	Act I	Act I	Act I
Second Week	Act I	Acts I–II	Act II	Acts I–II
Third Week	Act II	Acts II–III	Act III	Acts I–III
Fourth Week	Act III	Acts II–III	Acts I–III	Acts II–III
Fifth Week	Acts I–II–III	Acts I–II–III	Acts I–II–III	Acts I–II–III
Sixth Week	Acts I–II–III	Acts I–II–III	Acts I–II–III	Acts I–II–III

To remain on schedule, books should be dropped on Act I at the beginning of the second week, Act II at the beginning of the third week, and Act III at the beginning of the fourth week. Under the rotation plan, however, each actor had only five or six rehearsals on each act. rehearsals on each act of the play. That would surely be inadequate if it meant that each *actor* had only five or six rehearsals on each act. Under the rotation plan, however, each actor

REHEARSAL SCHEDULE

Rotation Casting

	Monday		**Tuesday**		**Wednesday**		**Thursday**	
First Week	Acts	Casts	Act	Casts	Act	Casts	Act	Casts
	I	A	I	A B	I	C D	I	A B
	II	B						
	III	C D						
Second Week	Acts	Casts	Acts	Casts	Act	Casts	Acts	Casts
	I	A B	I	C	II	C D	I	A
			II	A B			II	A B
Third Week	Act	Casts	Acts	Casts	Act	Casts	Acts	Casts
	II	C D	II	A	III	C D	I	B
			III	A B			III	A B
Fourth Week	Act	Casts	Acts	Casts	Acts	Casts	Acts	Casts
	III	C D	II	A B	I	C D	II	A C
			III	A	III	B	III	A B
Fifth Week	Acts	Cast	Acts	Cast	Acts	Cast	Acts	Cast
	I	A	I	B	I	C	I	D
	II	A	II	B	II	C	II	D
	III	A	III	B	III	C	III	D
Sixth Week	Acts	Cast	Acts	Cast	Acts	Cast	Acts	Cast
	I	A	I	B	I	C	I	D
	II	A	II	B	II	C	II	D
	III	A	III	B	III	C	III	D

appears in two casts—doubling his number of opportunities for rehearsal in the role.

If the entire last week is devoted to dress rehearsals, each actor will rehearse in costume and makeup twice before his first performance. He has the further advantage of seeing two dress rehearsals from the audience point of view and realizing something of the play's po-tential for stimulating involvement and response.

Performances, of course, follow the same rotation pattern. Actors can learn much by sitting in the audience and observing reactions during those performances when they do not appear onstage.

A SELECTED LIST OF PLAYS

Children's theatre by definition is theatre *for* children, not theatre *by* children, but some plays published for the children's theatre would be difficult to cast without including some small children and, therefore, are not well suited to production by youth theatre groups. The plays listed here were chosen because they can be done successfully by teen-age players.

Presenting such a list is not intended to suggest that every play mentioned is "easy to produce" or will be a good choice for every youth theatre. Differences in available talent, budget, and technical facilities as well as differences among audiences will guide each group to its own best selections.

The best way to know whether a play meets your needs is to read it. Each play listed here may be ordered from one of the following publishers:

Anchorage Press
Cloverlot
Anchorage, Kentucky 40223

Coach House Press, Inc.
53 West Jackson Boulevard
Chicago, Illinois 60604

David McKay Company, Inc.
750 Third Avenue
New York, N.Y. 10017

Dramatic Publishing Company
86 East Randolph Street
Chicago, Illinois 60601

Dramatists Play Service
440 Park Avenue South
New York, N.Y. 10016

I. E. Clark
Box 246
Schulenburg, Texas 78956

Modern Theatre for Youth
P.O. Box 10276
University Station
Denver, Colorado 80210

New Plays for Children
Box 2181, Grand Central Station
New York, N.Y. 10017

Samuel French, Inc.
25 West 45th Street
New York, N.Y. 10036

Title	*Author*	*Publisher*	*Cast*	*Royalty*
Abe Lincoln— New Salem Days	Charlotte Chorpenning	Coach House Press	9 Females 11 Males	$15.00
The Adventures of Tom Sawyer	Charlotte Chorpenning	Coach House Press	6 Females 14 Males	$15.00
Aesop's Fables	Ed Graczyk	Anchorage Press	13 or more	$25.00
Aladdin and the Wonderful Lamp	Elizabeth B. Dooley	Samuel French	8 (extras)	$ 5.00

Title	Author	Publisher	Cast	Royalty
Aladdin and the Wonderful Lamp	James Norris	Anchorage Press	4 Females 3 Males (2 extras)	$15.00
Ali Baba and the Forty Thieves	Wadeeha Atiyeh	Anchorage Press	3 Females 8 Males (1 donkey)	$15.00
Ali Baba and the Forty Thieves	Lillian and Robert Masters	Anchorage Press	3 Females 4 Males (extras)	$15.00
Alice in Wonderland	Charlotte Chorpenning	Coach House Press	18	$15.00
Alice in Wonderland	Alice Gerstenberg	David McKay Company	20	$25.00
Alice in Wonderland	Anne Martens	Dramatic Publishing Company	25	$15.00
Alice in Wonderland	Madge Miller	Anchorage Press	4 Females 2 Males (7 animals)	$15.00
Androcles and the Lion	Aurand Harris	Anchorage Press	1 Female 5 Males	$25.00
Arthur and the Magic Sword	Keith M. Engar	Anchorage Press	4 Females 12 Males	$15.00
Barnaby	Robert and Lillian Masters	Samuel French	5 Females 15 Males	$25.00
Beauty and the Beast	Ellen Stuart	New Plays for Children	5 Females 7 Males	$25.00
Beauty and the Beast	Jesse Beers, Jr.	Samuel French	10	$15.00
Beauty and the Beast	Nicholas Stuart Gray	Samuel French	7	$15.00
Beauty and the Beast	Nora McAlvay	Coach House Press	6 Females 5 Males	$15.00
The Beeple	Allan Cullen	Anchorage Press	6 Females 12 Males	$25.00
Big Klaus and Little Klaus	Dean Wenstrom	Anchorage Press	1 Female 6 Males (extras)	$25.00
The Brave Little Tailor	Aurand Harris	Anchorage Press	3 Females 3 Males	$15.00

Title	Author	Publisher	Cast	Royalty
Buffalo Bill	Aurand Harris	Anchorage Press	2 Females 15 Males (extras)	$15.00
The Canterville Ghost	Darwin Payne	Coach House Press	5 Females 3 Males	$15.00
The Cat on the Oregon Trail	Minta Meier	Coach House Press	8 Females 6 Males 1 Cat	$15.00
Cinderella	Charlotte Chorpenning	Anchorage Press	6 Females 4 Males	$15.00
Cinderella	Ruth Newton	Samuel French	12 (extras)	$10.00
Cinderella of Loreland	Frances Homer	Dramatic Publishing Company	12 Females 6 Males	$10.00 to $25.00
Circus in the Wind	Aurand Harris	Samuel French	2 Females 5 Males	$15.00
The Clown Who Ran Away	Conrad Seiler	David McKay Company	22	$15.00
The Cricket on the Hearth	Marian Johnson	Coach House Press	2 Females 5 Males 1 Dog	$15.00
The Dancing Donkey	Erik Vos	Anchorage Press	2 Females 3 Males (1 donkey)	$25.00
Daniel Boone	Leona Baptist	Anchorage Press	9 Females 9 Males	$15.00
David and Goliath	William Stock	New Plays for Children	1 Female 7 Males	$25.00
Davy Crockett and His Coonskin Cap	Margery Evernden	Coach House Press	3 Females 6 Males (1 Bear)	$15.00
Dick Whittington and His Cat	Lloyd Brady	Coach House Press	4 Females 8 Males (extras)	$15.00
Dick Whittington and His Cat	Ellen Stuart	New Plays for Children	5 Females 6 Males	$25.00
A Doctor in Spite of Himself	Aurand Harris	Anchorage Press	10 Females 9 Males	$15.00
Don Quixote of La Mancha	Arthur Fauquez	Anchorage Press	2 Females 8 Males (extras)	$25.00

Title	Author	Publisher	Cast	Royalty
The Elves and the Shoemaker	MacAlvay and Chorpenning	Anchorage Press	8 Females 1 Male (3 elves)	$15.00
The Emperor's New Clothes	Charlotte Chorpenning	Samuel French	4 Females 8 Males	$15.00
The Emperor's Nightingale	Madge Miller	Anchorage Press	3 Females 5 Males	$15.00
The Enchanted Treasure	Anne Nicholson	Coach House Press	1 Female 5 Males	$15.00
Flibbertygibbet, His Last Chance	Nora MacAlvay	Anchorage Press	4 Females 4 Males	$15.00
The Flying Prince	Aurand Harris	Samuel French	8 Females 7 Males	$15.00
The Frog Prince	Martha H. Newell	New Plays for Children	4 Females 1 Dancer	$25.00
The Frog Princess and the Witch	Margery Evernden	Coach House Press	5 Females 6 Males	$15.00
The Golden Sandals	Ellen Stuart	New Plays for Children	4 Females 6 Males (extras)	$25.00
Good Grief, A Griffin	Eleanor and Ray Harder	Anchorage Press	5 Females 7 Males	$25.00
The Great Cross-Country Race	Alan Broadhurst	Anchorage Press	6 Females 5 Males	$25.00
Greensleeves' Magic	Marian Johnson	Coach House Press	5 Females 6 Males (extras)	$15.00
Hansel and Gretel	Madge Miller	Anchorage Press	4 Females 2 Males (extras)	$15.00
Hiawatha, Peacemaker of the Iroquois	James Norris	Anchorage Press	3 Females 13 Males	$15.00
The Hobbit	Patricia Gray	Dramatic Publishing Company	Flexible	$25.00
The House at Pooh Corner	Bettye Knapp	Dramatic Publishing Company	1 Male 10 Animals	$25.00
Huckleberry Finn	Frank Whiting	Anchorage Press	6 Females 12 Males	$25.00

Title	Author	Publisher	Cast	Royalty
The Ice Wolf	Joanna Kraus	New Plays for Children	7 Females 8 Males	$25.00
Indian Captive: The Story of Mary Jemison	Lois Lenski	Coach House Press	12 Females 7 Males (extras)	$25.00
Jack and the Beanstalk	Charlotte Chorpenning	Anchorage Press	6 Females 7 Males (extras)	$15.00
Jack and the Beanstalk	Elenore Parker	New Plays for Children	2 Females 3 Males 1 Child	$25.00
Jack and the Giant	Ruth Newton	Samuel French	10 (extras)	$10.00
Joan of Arc	Anne Nicholson	Coach House Press	4 Females 8 Males	$15.00
Johnny Moonbeam and the Silver Arrow	Joseph Golden	Anchorage Press	5 Males (extras)	$15.00
King Arthur's Sword	Margery Evernden	Coach House Press	2 Females 6 Males	$15.00
The King of the Golden River	John Ruskin	Coach House Press	3 Females 5 Males	$15.00
The Knave of Hearts	Louise Saunders	David McKay Company	15	$10.00
The Land of the Dragon	Madge Miller	Anchorage Press	5 Females 3 Males (1 dragon)	$15.00
The Land of Oz	Elizabeth Fuller Goodspeed	Samuel French	22 (extras)	$25.00
Lincoln's Secret Messenger	Charlotte Chorpenning	Coach House Press	13 Females 12 Males	$15.00
Little Lee Bobo	Lee and Charlotte Chorpenning	Anchorage Press	19 Females 2 Males	$15.00
The Little Mermaid	Pat Hale	New Plays for Children	8 Females 5 Males	$25.00
Little Women	Sara Spencer	Anchorage Press	10 Females 2 Males	$15.00
McGillicuddy McGotham	Leonard Wibberly	Dramatic Publishing Company	Flexible	$10.00

Title	Author	Publisher	Cast	Royalty
The Magic Horn of Charlemagne	Nicholson and Chorpenning	Coach House Press	5 Females 7 Males	$15.00
Magic in the Sky	Norma Langham	Coach House Press	5 Females 9 Males	$15.00
The Magic Isle	Tassel and Ollington	Modern Theatre for Youth	9	$25.00
Make-Believe	A. A. Milne	Samuel French	30	$25.00
The Man in the Moon	Alan Cullen	Anchorage Press	5 Females 8 Males	$25.00
The Man Who Killed Time	Arthur Fauquez	Anchorage Press	4 Females 5 Males	$25.00
Many Moons	Charlotte Chorpenning	Dramatic Publishing Company	5 Females 5 Males	$25.00
Marco Polo	Geraldine Siks	Anchorage Press	3 Females 9 Males	$15.00
The Marvelous Land of Oz	Adele Thane	Anchorage Press	2 Females 6 Males	$15.00
Mean to Be Free	Joanna Kraus	New Plays for Children	4 Females 10 Males	$25.00
The Merry Pranks of Tyll	Daniel Fleischhacker	Anchorage Press	6 Females 11 Males	$15.00
Mrs. McThing	Mary Chase	Dramatists Play Service	10 Females 9 Males	$50.00 to $25.00
Names and Nicknames	James Reaney	New Plays for Children	2 Females 4 Males	$25.00
New Clothes for the Emperor	Nicholas Stuart Gray	Samuel French	3 Females 11 Males	$15.00
Niccolo and Nicolette	Alan Cullen	Anchorage Press	3 Females 7 Males	$25.00
The Nuremberg Stove	Geraldine Siks	Anchorage Press	5 Females 7 Males	$15.00
Oliver Twist	Muriel Browne	Anchorage Press	5 Females 8 Males	$15.00
The Patchwork Girl of Oz	Mary L. Marshall	Samuel French	19	$15.00
Pegora the Witch	Carol Wright	Anchorage Press	10 Females 6 Males (extras)	$15.00
Peter Pan	J. M. Barrie	Samuel French	25	$35.00

Title	Author	Publisher	Cast	Royalty
The Pied Piper of Hamelin	Madge Miller	Anchorage Press	4 Females 5 Males (extras)	$15.00
Pinocchio and the Indians	Aurand Harris	Samuel French	13	$15.00
The Plain Princess	Aurand Harris	Anchorage Press	7 Females 4 Males (extras)	$15.00
Pocohontas	Aurand Harris	Anchorage Press	2 Females 5 Males	$15.00
Prince Fairyfoot	Geraldine Brain Siks	Anchorage Press	3 Females 5 Males	$15.00
The Prince and the Pauper	Charlotte Chorpenning	Anchorage Press	10 Females 16 Males	$15.00
The Princess and the Swineherd	Madge Miller	Anchorage Press	5 Females 3 Males	$15.00
Rags to Riches	Aurand Harris	Anchorage Press	3 Females 5 Males (extras)	$25.00
Rama and the Tigers	Charlotte Chorpenning	Coach House Press	1 Female 2 Males 9 Animals	$15.00
Ransom of Red Chief	Anne Martens	Dramatic Publishing Company	5 Females 9 Males	$15.00
Rapunzel and the Witch	Jack Melanos	Anchorage Press	3 Females 2 Males	$15.00
The Red Shoes	Robin Short	Samuel French	3 Females 3 Males (extras)	$15.00
Remi's Secret Locket	Burger and DeBear	Coach House Press	3 Females 8 Males (extras)	$15.00
Reynard the Fox	Arthur Fauquez	Anchorage Press	1 Female 6 Males	$25.00
Rip Van Winkle	Charlotte Chorpenning	Coach House Press	11 Females 10 Males (extras)	$15.00
Robin Hood	James Norris	Anchorage Press	2 Females 9 Males	$15.00

Title	Author	Publisher	Cast	Royalty
Robinson Crusoe	Charlotte Chorpenning	Anchorage Press	2 Females 4 Males (extras)	$15.00
Rumpelstiltskin	Charlotte Chorpenning	Anchorage Press	5 Females 6 Males	$15.00
Rumpelstiltskin	Margery Evernden	Coach House Press	2 Females 5 Males (extras)	$15.00
The Secret of Han Ho	Margery Evernden	Coach House Press	1 Female 11 Males (extras)	$15.00
Simple Simon	Aurand Harris	Anchorage Press	4 Females 7 Males (extras)	$15.00
Sinbad the Sailor	Jack Melanos	Anchorage Press	5 Females 7 Males	$15.00
Sing Ho for a Prince	Joe Grenzeback	Coach House Press	13 Females 15 Males	$15.00
The Sleeping Beauty	Charlotte Chorpenning	Anchorage Press	12 Females 5 Males	$15.00
Sleeping Beauty of Loreland	Frances Homer	Dramatic Publishing Company	12 Females 6 Males	$10.00 to $25.00
The Snow Queen and the Goblin	Martha King	Coach House Press	3 Females 4 Males (extras)	$15.00
Snow White and the Seven Dwarfs	Jessie Braham White	Samuel French	24	$25.00
Snow White and the Seven Dwarfs	Marian Jonson	Coach House Press	7 Females 10 Males	$15.00
Sorcerer's Apprentice	Anne Martens	Dramatic Publishing Company	3 Females 2 Males (extras)	$15.00
Tanuki, the Mischievous Raccoon	Clive Rickabaugh	Coach House Press	6 Females 5 Males	$15.00
The Tinder Box	Alan Broadhurst	Anchorage Press	4 Females 8 Males (extras)	$25.00
The Tinder Box	Nicholas Stuart Gray	Samuel French	19	$15.00

Title	Author	Publisher	Cast	Royalty
The Tingalary Bird	Mary Melwood	New Plays for Children	2 Females 2 Males	$25.00
Toad of Toad Hall	A. A. Milne	Samuel French	8 Females 19 Males	$25.00
Tom Sawyer	Paul Kester	Samuel French	21	$25.00
Tom Sawyer	Sarah Schlesinger	New Plays for Children	7 Females 8 Males	$25.00
Tom Sawyer's Treasure Hunt	Charlotte Chorpenning	Samuel French	21	$25.00
Treasure Island	Dorothy Drew	Anchorage Press	1 Female 14 Males	$15.00
Twelve Dancing Princesses	I. E. Clark	I. E. Clark	15 Females 4 Males	$25.00
Two Pails of Water	Aad Greidanus	Anchorage Press	2 Females 4 Males	$25.00
Tyl Eulenspiegel and the Talking Donkey	Robert and Lillian Masters	Coach House Press	5 Females 10 Males (extras)	$15.00
The Unwicked Witch	Madge Miller	Anchorage Press	4 Females 2 Males	$15.00
The Wind in the Willows	Kenneth Grahame	Dramatic Publishing Company	Flexible	$25.00
Winnie the Pooh	A. A. Milne	Dramatic Publishing Company	Flexible	$25.00
Wizard of Oz	Elizabeth F. Goodspeed	Samuel French	14 (extras)	$25.00
The Wizard of Oz	Anne Martens	Dramatic Publishing Company	13 Females 8 Males (extras)	$15.00
The Wizard of Oz	Adele Thane	Anchorage Press	7 Females 6 Males (extras)	$15.00
The Wizard of Oz	Camilla Wolak	New Plays for Children	4 Females 5 Males (extras)	$25.00
The Wonderful Tang	Beaumont Bruestle	Anchorage Press	6 Females 8 Males (extras)	$15.00
Yankee Doodle Comes to Town	Martha Bennett King	Coach House Press	5 Females 7 Males	$15.00

Title	Author	Publisher	Cast	Royalty
Young Ben Franklin's Fight for Freedom	Faye Parker	Coach House Press	2 Females 6 Males (extras)	$15.00
Young Dick Whittington	Alan Broadhurst	Anchorage Press	5 Females 12 Males (extras)	$25.00
Young Hickory	Helen McKenna	Anchorage Press	3 Females 11 Males	$15.00

SOURCES OF SUPPLY

The most readily available reference in seeking out distributors of theatre supplies probably will be any or all of the periodicals listed in the Bibliography. Their advertisers generally offer catalogues so that, by sending off a few postcards, you will be able to do some comparison shopping.

Of course, the Yellow Pages in the telephone directory will indicate whether there are suppliers of theatre materials in your own community. Having a local source for expendable items is a great convenience.

Some kinds of material not usually listed as theatre supplies but that have been cited as useful in this book may be more difficult to find by the usual means. Specific sources for them, therefore, are listed below.

Fittings for Pipe Construction

Holleander Manufacturing Company
3841 Spring Grove Avenue
Cincinnati, Ohio 45223

Kee Klamps North America Limited
79 Benors Drive
Buffalo, New York 14225

Mutual Hardware Corporation
5–45 49th Avenue
Long Island City, New York 11101

Up-Right Scaffolds
6677 Northwest Highway
Chicago, Illinois 60631

Plastics

Cadillac Plastic and Chemical Company
15111 Second Avenue
Detroit, Michigan 48203

Chemical Marketing
5117 N. Clark Street
Chicago, Illinois 60640

Insto-Foam Midwest
P.O. Box 287
Waukegan, Illinois 60085

Midway Industrial Supply Company
978 Raymond Avenue
St. Paul, Minnesota 55114

Northwest Fiberglas Supply, Inc.
3055 Columbia Avenue N.E.
Minneapolis, Minnesota 55418

Plastics, Inc.
224 Ryan Avenue
St. Paul, Minnesota 55102

Instructional Film Strips

Oleson Company
1535 Ivor Avenue
Hollywood, California 90028

Paramount Theatrical Supplies
32 West 20th Street
New York, N.Y. 10011

BIBLIOGRAPHY

Books on Acting

Alberti, Eva. *A Handbook of Acting: Based in the New Pantomime by Madame Eva Alberti, Edited by R. Hyndman.* Samuel French, New York, 1932.

Boleslavski, Richard. *Acting: The First Six Lessons.* Theatre Arts, New York, 1933.

Chekhov, Michael. *To the Actor: On the Technique of Acting.* Harper & Row, New York, 1953.

Cole, Toby. *Acting: A Handbook of the Stanislavsky Method.* Crown, New York, 1955.

—————. *Actors on Acting: The Theories, Techniques, and Practices of the Great Actors of All Times as Told in Their Own Words.* Crown, New York, 1961.

A Course Guide in the Theatre Arts at the Secondary School Level. American Educational Theatre Association, Washington, D.C., 1968.

Funke, Lewis. *Actors Talk About Acting: Fourteen Interviews with Stars of the Theatre.* Random House, New York, 1961.

Goodman, Edward. *Make Believe: The Art of Acting.* Charles Scribner's Sons, New York, 1956.

McGaw, Charles. *Acting Is Believing: A Basic Method for Beginners.* Holt, Rinehart & Winston, New York, 1966.

Rawson, Ruth. *The Theatre Student: Acting.* Richards Rosen Press, New York, 1970.

Selden, Samuel. *First Steps in Acting.* Appleton-Century-Crofts, New York, 1964.

Spolin, Viola. *Improvisation for the Theatre: A Handbook of Teaching and Directing Techniques.* Northwestern University, Evanston, Illinois, 1963.

Stanislavsky, Constantin S. *An Actor Prepares.* Theatre Arts, New York, 1936.

—————. *An Actor's Handbook.* Theatre Arts, New York, 1963.

—————. *Building a Character.* Theatre Arts, New York, 1949.

—————. *Creating a Role.* Theatre Arts, New York, 1961.

Books on Children's Theatre

Allen, John. *Play Production with Children and Young People.* Dennis Dobson, London.

Birner, William B. *Twenty Plays for Young People.* Anchorage Press, Anchorage, Kentucky, 1967.

Chorpenning, Charlotte. *Twenty-One Years with Children's Theatre.* Anchorage Press, Chicago, Illinois, 1954.

Davis, Jed H. and Mary Jane Watkins. *Children's Theatre: Play Production for the Child Audience.* Harper & Row, New York, 1960.

Forkert, Otto Maurice. *Children's Theatre that Captures Its Audience.* Coach House Press, Chicago, 1962.

Johnson, Richard C. *Theatre for Children.* National Thespian Society, Cincinnati, 1966.

Kase, Robert C. *Children's Theatre Comes of Age: For Schools, Colleges and Community Theatres.* Samuel French, New York, 1956.

Seattle Junior Programs, Inc. *Children's Theatre Manual: A Guide for the Organization and Operation of a Non-Profit Community Children's Theatre, Compiled by Seattle Junior Programm, Inc.* Children's Theatre Press, Chicago, 1951.

Siks, Geraldine Brain and Hazel B. Dunnington. *Children's Theatre and Creative Dramatics.* University of Washington, Seattle, 1961.

Slade, Peter. *Child Drama.* University of London, London, 1954.

Ward, Winifred. *Theatre for Children.* Children's Theatre Press, Chicago, 1950.

Books on Creativity and Creative Drama

Burger, Isabel B. *Creative Play Acting: Learning Through Drama.* Ronald Press, New York, 1950.

Fitzgerald, Burdette S. *World Tales for Creative Dramatics and Storytelling.* Prentice-Hall, Englewood Cliffs, N.J., 1962.

Kase, Robert C. *Stories for Creative Acting: Stories Recommended and Used Successfully by Leading Creative Dramatics, Directors and Teachers.* Samuel French, New York, 1961.

Mearns, Hughes. *Creative Power: The Education of Youth in the Creative Arts.* Dover, New York, 1958.

Siks, Geraldine Brain. *Children's Literature for Dramatization.* Harper & Row, New York, 1964.

——————. *Creative Dramatics: An Art for Children.* Harper & Row, New York, 1958.

Ward, Winifred. *Playmaking with Children: From Kindergarten Through Junior High School.* Appleton-Century-Crofts, New York, 1953.

——————. *Stories to Dramatize.* Children's Theatre Press, Chicago, 1952.

Books on Costume

Barton, Lucy. *Costumes by You: Eight Essays for Experience.* Walter Baker, Boston, 1940.

——————. *Historic Costume for the Stage.* Walter Baker, Boston, 1935.

——————. *Period Patterns: A Supplement to Historic Costume for the Stage.* Walter Baker, Boston, 1942.

Berk, Barbara. *The First Book of Stage Costume and Make-Up.* Franklin Watts, New York, 1954.

Bruhn, Wolfgang. *A Pictorial History of Costume: A Survey of Costume of All Periods and Peoples from Antiquity to Modern Times Including National Costume in Europe and Non-European Countries.* Praeger, New York, 1955.

Corson, Richard. *Fashions in Hair: The First 5000 Years.* Hastings House, New York, 1965.

Prisk, Bernice and Robert Byers, *The Theatre Student: Costuming.* Richards Rosen Press, New York, 1969.

Payne, Blanche. *History of Costume: From the Ancient Egyptians to the Twentieth Century,* Harper & Row, New York, 1965.

Snook, Barbara. *Costumes for School Plays.* B. T. Batsford, London, 1965.

Tilke, Max. *Costume Patterns and Designs: A Survey of Costume Patterns and Designs of All Periods and Nations from Antiquity to Modern Times.* Praeger, New York, 1957.

Walkup, Fairfax Proudfit. *Dressing the Part: A History of Costume for the Theatre.* Appleton-Century-Crofts, New York, 1950.

White, A. V. *Making Stage Costumes for Amateurs.* Routledge & Kegan Paul, London, 1957.

Books on Directing

Cole, Toby. *Directors on Directing.* Bobbs-Merrill, Indianapolis, 1963.

Hopkins, Arthur. *Reference Point.* Samuel French, New York, 1948.

Kozelka, Paul. *The Theatre Student: Directing.* Richards Rosen Press, New York, 1968.

Spolin, Viola. *Improvisation for the Theatre: A Handbook of Teaching and Directing Techniques.* Northwestern University, Evanston, Illinois, 1963.

Books on Stage Lighting

Bongar, Emmet. *The Theatre Student: Practical Stage Lighting.* Richards Rosen, New York, 1971.

Fuchs, Theodore. *Home-Built Lighting Equipment for the Small Stage.* Samuel French, New York, 1939.

——————. *Stage Lighting,* Ben Blom, New York, 1963.

McCandless, Stanley. *A Method of Lighting the Stage.* Theatre Arts, New York, 1958.

Rubin, Joel. *Theatrical Lighting Practice.* Theatre Arts, New York, 1954.

Wilfred, Thomas. *Projected Scenery: A Technical Manual.* Drama Book Shop, New York, 1965.

Books on Stage Makeup

Baird, John F. *Make-Up: A Manual for the Use of Actors, Amateur and Professional.* Samuel French, New York, 1957.

Corey, Irene. *The Mask of Reality.* Anchorage Press, Anchorage, Kentucky, 1968.

Corson, Richard. *Stage Make-Up.* Appleton-Century-Crofts, New York, 1960.

Johnson, Richard C. and Robert Seaver. *Make-Up for the Stage* (film strip and text). Paramount Theatrical Supplies, New York, 1955.

Books on Stagecraft

Adix, Vern. *Theatre Scenecraft: For the Backstage Technician and Artist.* Children's Theatre Press, Anchorage, Kentucky, 1956.

Gillette, A. S. *Stage Scenery: Its Construction and Rigging.* Harper & Row, New York, 1959.

Hake, Herbert V. *Here's How: A Basic Stagecraft Book.* Row, Peterson, Evanston, Illinois, 1958.

Nelms, Henning. *A Primer of Stagecraft.* Dramatist, New York, 1955.

Southern, Richard. *Stage Settings for Amateurs and Professionals.* Theatre Arts, New York, 1960.

Stell, W. Joseph. *The Theatre Student: Scenery.* Richards Rosen Press, New York, 1970.

Books on Theatre

Allen, John. *Going to the Theatre.* Phoenix House Ltd., London, 1952.

——————. *Great Moments in the Theatre.* Roy Publishers, New York, 1958.

Ernst, Earle. *The Kabuki Theatre.* Oxford, New York, 1956.

Green, Stanley. *The World of Musical Comedy.* Grosset & Dunlap, New York, 1962.

Selden, Samuel. *Man in His Theatre.* University of North Carolina, Chapel Hill, 1957.

Whiting, Frank M. *An Introduction to the Theatre.* Harper and Brothers, New York, 1961.

Wright, Edward A. *A Primer for Playgoers: An Introduction to the Understanding and Appreciation of Cinema-Stage-Television.* Prentice-Hall, Englewood Cliffs, N.J., 1958.

Useful Periodicals

Children's Theatre Review. American Educational Theatre Association, Washington, D.C.

Dramatics. International Thespian Society, Cincinnati, Ohio.

Players. Northern Illinois University, DeKalb, Illinois.

The Secondary School Theatre. American Educational Theatre Association, Washington, D.C.

Theatre Crafts. Rodale Press, New York.